Surrender

A Memoir of Letting Go and Beginning Again

✦ ✦ ✦

by Nobody

THE
NOBODY
COLLECTIVE

Surrender – by Nobody

This book is a work of nonfiction based on the author's memories,
experiences, and reflections. Some names and identifying details
have been changed to protect the privacy of individuals.

First Edition-2025 Printed in the United States of America

Library of Congress Control Number: 2025917260

ISBN: 979-8-9997846-1-2 (Paperback Edition)
ISBN: 979-8-9997846-2-9 (E-book Edition)

Published by The Nobody Collective

THE
NOBODY
COLLECTIVE

*The Nobody Collective is an independent publishing imprint
dedicated to works of honesty, healing, and surrender.*

Dedication

✦ ✦ ✦

To F— For the love that woke something in me I didn't even know was sleeping. You didn't just change my heart—you rearranged my entire inner world.

Because of you, this book was born. Not out of revenge. Not out of bitterness. But out of the silence you left behind—a silence so loud, it had to become something.

You were the reason I started writing. Trying to understand. Trying to remember. Trying to let go.

You were the spark that lit the most beautiful fire—and the ache that burned long after the flame was gone. You were the almost, the what-if, the love that never found a place to land.

And though everything looks different now, we're still here—still in each other's world in quieter, gentler ways. Not as we were, but as we are now: two people who walked through something beautiful, something hard, and came out changed—but still connected.

Your imprint is in every chapter— not as a villain, not as a hero, but as the boy I loved too much, the goodbye I never wanted to say, the lesson I didn't know I needed.

To the ones who almost gave up. And to the ones who still believe. You are the reason I kept writing.

This book is for you.

For every heart that's ever broken in silence. For every soul that rebuilt itself in the dark.

This is for you. And for me.

To the ones who left, and the ones who stayed. To Marie, who became a lighthouse in my storm. And to the stranger reading this—I hope you find your way home.

This is for you.

"When love breaks you open, let it.
That's where the light begins to enter."

Author's Note

✦ ✦ ✦

This is not the story I ever imagined I would tell. And certainly not like this—this exposed, this honest, this raw

I never set out to write a book. I set out to survive.

What you're holding isn't just a collection of memories—it's a map. A map through heartbreak, identity, loss, and the long road back to myself. These pages were born in the quietest moments, when everything else had fallen apart—written in the nights when sleep never came, in the mornings when grief made it hard to breathe, and in the stillness where silence became unbearable.

I didn't write this for attention. I wrote it because I had nowhere else to put the pain. Because healing doesn't always look like light or clarity. Sometimes, it looks like trembling hands on a keyboard and a heart breaking open on the page.

This book is not about blame. It's not about heroes or villains. It's about what it means to feel deeply, to unravel, to lose yourself in love, and to slowly—painfully—begin again. It's about the moments we don't post. The thoughts we don't admit. The ghosts we carry long after the doors have closed.

You won't find perfect closure here. There are no clean lines or easy answers. Just truth. Just emotion. Just the raw, unfiltered journey of a person learning to let go—not only of others, but of expectations, of illusions, of old versions of self.

If you've ever loved too much, trusted too quickly, stayed too long, or questioned your worth—this is for you. If you've ever felt like too much, not enough, or somewhere lost in between—this is for you. If you've ever been invisible, heartbroken, or lost in a life you didn't recognize—this is for you.

And if you're still trying to find your way back to yourself— I hope this reminds you: You are not alone.

Thank you for holding space for my truth. I hope, in some small way, it helps you feel less alone in yours.

"These pages were born of pain, but they carry hope too— that even in the dark, we can find our way back to ourselves."

With everything, **Nobody - Mariusz Podkalicki**

Contents

✦ ✦ ✦

Introduction – When the Breaking Point Becomes the Beginning..........1

Chapter 1 The Trigger, the Day I Let Go.....................................5

Chapter 2 The Lie Called Maybe 8

Chapter 3 How It All Started — The Beginning of an End.................13

Chapter 4 The First Yes...18

Chapter 5 The Goodbye That Came Too Soon 24

Chapter 6 Holding On Across the Distance 27

Chapter 7 Orlando – A Different Kind of Beginning......................30

Chapter 8 Where the Magic Felt Real..36

Chapter 9 Magic Continued 40

Chapter 10 After the Magic 44

Chapter 11 Hope's Last Spark..50

Chapter 12 Miami – The Almost...53

Chapter 13 Borrowed Words..62

Chapter 14 Almost Home...67

Chapter 15 Almost isn't enough 77

Chapter 16 What I Thought It Meant 82

Chapter 17 Dressed in Hope, Left in Silence 88

Chapter 18 The Days After – Grieving Someone Still Alive 94

Chapter 19 The Ghost Season 97

Chapter 20 Crypto, Catfish, and the Cost of Loneliness.................103

Chapter 21 When Hope Becomes a Weapon 107

Chapter 22 When It All Made Sense..110

Chapter 23 What Was Left After Everything Ended............................116

Chapter 24 The Space I Tried to Fill..123

Chapter 25 The Night I Stopped Chasing Love...................................131

Chapter 26 Before Pride, There Was Pain..137

Chapter 27 When the Mind Breaks and the Body Follows 142

Chapter 28 The Love That Stayed..147

Chapter 29 Learning to Understand Myself… and Him 152

Chapter 30 The Love That Asked for Nothing....................................156

Chapter 31 When They Leave – Fractured Friendships and
            Those Who Stayed 160

Chapter 32 The Hardest Truth Is the One We Already Know 165

Chapter 33 A Language That Found Me...169

Chapter 34 A Vacation, A Spark, A Light..173

Chapter 35 Pink Dragon 177

Chapter 36 Mirror Wars..184

Chapter 37 The Grass Is Not Always Greener on the Other Side.......190

Chapter 38 My Sanctuary 198

Chapter 39 Mother Ayahuasca: The Call Back to Myself....................203

Chapter 40 They Didn't Have to—But They Did, Because
            They Chose Love..211

Chapter 41 Time to Say Goodbye – Love Letter to a City
            That Never Stayed...216

Chapter 42 Let the Garden Bloom..222

Epilogue – The Garden After the Storm 227

Acknowledgments...229

About the Author..231

Thank You..233

Resources 235

Surrender

by Nobody

"I spent so long feeling like nobody—unseen, unheard, forgotten. But in the silence of my pain, I wrote. And through every word, I stitched myself back together. I didn't just find my voice—I found me."

Mariusz Podkalicki

Introduction

When the Breaking Point Becomes the Beginning

*"You don't always hear the sound of your breaking—
until the silence that follows feels louder than life."*

Everyone has a moment when they break. Mine came quietly—and all at once.

I had spent years holding it all in—grief, fear, heartbreak, shame—like water cupped in trembling hands, praying none would spill. I thought if I stayed strong, kept smiling, kept hoping, maybe life would fall back into place. Maybe love would return. Maybe safety would find me again.

But life doesn't reward silent endurance. The pain you avoid will always find its way back.

When it all came crashing down—my job, my health, my sense of self, and the person I loved most—I was left standing in the wreckage, hollow and unrecognizable, no longer knowing who I was without the very things I had fought so hard to hold onto.

It didn't feel like a breakthrough. It felt like a breakdown—a slow, quiet collapse of everything I'd built around me. And yet, it was in that collapse that something shifted. The fight was gone. The pretending was over. I had no choice but to face what was left—just me, stripped bare.

I was drowning in a life that no longer fit me. This book was born from that place.

It's not a manual for healing. It's not a tidy redemption arc. It's a raw, unfiltered collection of moments—of loving too much, losing everything, and discovering that letting go doesn't mean giving up. Sometimes, it means choosing yourself for the very first time.

I wrote this for anyone who has cried alone in the dark, wondering if they'll ever feel whole again. For anyone who's felt like too much and not enough in the same breath. For anyone who's loved deeply, lost silently, and stood in the ruins of the life they thought they'd have, unsure how to begin again.

And I wrote it for myself, too.

This is not a how-to. It's a heart cracked open. A hand reaching out. A voice saying, *"I've been there. And I made it through."*

This is for you.

Because I know what it's like to break. I know what it's like to lose the person you thought would never let go. To hide your pain. To wear strength like armor. To hope so hard it hurts.

But I also know this: You are allowed to let go. You are allowed to fall apart. You are allowed to begin again.

This is my story…

And maybe, somewhere in these pages, you'll find pieces of your own—fragments of moments you thought you'd buried, echoes of love you still ache for, the quiet weight of unspoken goodbyes. You might see your heartbreak mirrored in mine, your unanswered questions, your nights spent staring at the ceiling, wondering if you'll ever feel like yourself again.

You may stumble upon memories you thought had faded, feelings you didn't realize still lived inside you. And perhaps you'll find the words you didn't know you needed—the ones that remind you you're not weak for hurting, and you're not broken beyond repair.

As you turn these pages, I hope you see your own small victories taking shape, your own moments of courage rising from the shadows, and the faint flicker of something you thought you'd lost—hope.

And when you see yourself here, in these scattered pieces, I hope you feel less alone. Because there is no single, perfect way to heal—only your way.

This isn't just my story of breaking — it's my story of beginning again.

"Sometimes, the moment you break is the moment you begin."

Chapter 1

The Trigger, the Day I Let Go

*"Sometimes it's not the thunder that breaks
you—it's the silence after."*

It didn't happen in some grand, cinematic moment. It happened on a Tuesday afternoon, on my couch, in the smallest of silences—when the weight I had carried for years finally became too heavy to pretend I could hold.

I was sitting there, legs curled beneath me, a half-empty mug of cold coffee on the table. The TV was on, but the voices were nothing more than a dull hum—blurry shapes moving across the screen I couldn't bring myself to focus on. My phone lit up now and then with messages I didn't have the energy to answer.

The air felt heavy, as if the room itself had been holding its breath along with me. I stared at the same spot on the wall. Minutes. Maybe hours.

My chest was heavy, my arms limp, my heartbeat slow and tired in the quiet. There was no sharp pain, no sudden swell of emotion. Just emptiness. That deep, hollow kind of hopelessness where even breathing feels like work.

And then it happened. It wasn't gradual. One moment—I was still. The next—my vision blurred, my lips trembled, my shoulders began to shake before I even knew why.

The tears came hard and fast, as if something inside me had split open without warning. My breath caught in my throat. I gasped, like I'd been underwater too long. I buried my face in my hands, but it didn't stop—

The sobs kept coming, raw and unrelenting. It wasn't just sadness. It was everything. All the grief I'd swallowed, the heartbreak I'd never named, the shame I'd worn like a second skin.

Years of silent endurance, buried so deep I thought I'd forgotten them—now rushing through me like floodwater breaking a dam. My mind told me to hold it together. My body had already let go.

That day, it all came pouring out—grief, heartbreak, disappointment, unworthiness, sorrow—like a waterfall I couldn't control. The pain wasn't new. I had been living with it quietly, letting it carve into me day after day. But that day, I couldn't pretend anymore.

My life was falling apart—every piece of it. Loss of a job. Health problems. Financial struggles. Fractured relationships. Heartbreak.

Everything came almost at once, and it hit like lightning. I was not ready for the storm. I could handle the rain. But when the thunder roared and everything struck at once, I shattered—like a wooden stick crushed under full weight.

No pressure anymore. Just the snap. And it left me bleeding.

That was my turning point. I realized I couldn't keep forcing anything—not love, not healing, not people to stay. I had been chasing something that wasn't meant for me, clinging to a fantasy, hoping that if I just held on tighter, it would become real. But it never did.

The truth is, when you hold on to pain for so long, there's no room for anything else. I had been holding sadness so tightly that there was no space left for joy. No opening for peace—the one thing I craved—it couldn't find a way in.

I thought I was surviving. But I was slowly disappearing.

Once, I was the one trying to save everyone else.

I stayed up until sunrise listening to heartbreaks that weren't mine, holding hands through tears I didn't cause, carrying pain I couldn't fix—but couldn't bear to leave alone.

The one who stayed on the phone for hours, talking someone back from their own edge—even when I was standing at mine.

I was the steady one. The rescuer. The safe place everyone else could collapse into.

And then—suddenly—I found myself on the other side, needing someone to save me. The one holding onto the edge with trembling hands, silently praying someone would notice before I slipped.

But I was too proud, too afraid, too ashamed to ask for help. I didn't want to take up space in someone else's storm. I didn't want to become the weight in anyone's already-heavy hands. I felt like a burden.

So I hid. Hoping it would all go away.

But the real world doesn't work like that. No one came. No one could.

I was left alone, surrounded by the wreckage, with only myself to pick up the pieces. And in the quiet of that brokenness, I realized something powerful: I was the only one who could save me...

I didn't know it then, but falling apart was the only way I would ever come back whole. And in the silence after the breaking, I finally heard the sound of my own heartbeat—still strong.

In losing everything, I realized the only person who could save me... was me.

✦ ✦ ✦

"Letting go didn't feel like strength. It felt like surrender.
But that was the moment I began to heal."

Chapter 2

The Lie Called Maybe

*"Hope is the most dangerous ghost— it keeps
you company while it haunts you."*

Still, there was one thing I hadn't let go of: hope.
A small, flickering hope for the love of my life—F.—the person I had been silently holding space for, guarding like a secret I didn't dare set free. I told myself that maybe, one day, he'd see me the way I saw him— not just as a person, but as a whole universe I wanted to live in.

I saw him in colors I didn't know how to name. In the light that caught his face when he smiled. In the way his voice could steady me without even trying.

I saw the quiet thoughtfulness in his eyes, the boyish mischief that appeared when he forgot to guard himself, the kindness he gave away without ever asking for it back. To me, he wasn't just someone I loved—he was a place. A place I could breathe. A place I wanted to come home to, again and again, for the rest of my life.

And maybe…

The Thread That Hurts

Maybe was the soft place I landed when the truth felt too sharp. Maybe was the thread I wrapped around my fingers so I wouldn't feel empty-handed. Maybe became the air I breathed when the silence between us grew too loud.

Maybe kept me there. I had built a life around maybe.

Maybe he just needed time. Maybe if I showed up differently. Maybe I wasn't enough yet—but I could be. Maybe the timing would finally be right. Maybe it wasn't really over. Maybe what we once had—what we lost—could be found again.

It was easier to live inside the fantasy of a future that might still happen than to confront the reality that it wouldn't. Maybe gave me a thread to hold when everything else had slipped through my hands.

I lived inside the rhythm of maybe. Because maybe was easier than never. Maybe was gentler than gone. And maybe—was all I had left.

But maybe is a trickster. It whispers just enough to keep you from leaving. It comforts you with a lie dressed as hope. And I believed it. I fed it. I nurtured it like it was a seed that might someday bloom.

Every unanswered message. Every half-smile that didn't quite reach his eyes. Every memory we ever made—

The night we danced for hours under the open sky on the Fire Island beach during the Pines Party. The moment the sun began to rise and the rain poured down on us, soaking our clothes, our skin, and still—we kept dancing. The nights we curled up on the couch, tangled together, watching movies like the rest of the world had disappeared. The way he stood in my doorway on our first Valentine's Day, holding flowers, looking at me like I was exactly where he wanted to be.

I kept them all. Not just to remember him, but to remember us— the way it felt when he was still mine, when I still believed he would always be.

They became breadcrumbs I followed back to a place that didn't exist anymore, a map to a home that was gone, but one I kept looking for anyway.

I stitched them into a story where the ending hadn't been written yet. Where love still had a chance. Where maybe still meant something.

But the truth was already there. I just didn't want to read it.

The Question I Didn't Want to Ask

Some days, I knew deep down F. had moved on. I could feel it in the way he stopped asking how I was. In the way he responded just a little too slowly. In the way his presence grew quieter each time we spoke.

He wasn't pulling away all at once—he was fading. Gently. Almost kindly. And that's what hurt the most. It didn't feel cruel. It felt final.

Still, I didn't stop hoping. Because the moment I stopped hoping, I would have to grieve. And I wasn't ready.

Grieving would mean accepting that I had loved someone who didn't love me back in the same way. It would mean admitting that I wasn't the exception. That I wouldn't be the one he came back for.

So I stayed in maybe. Maybe became my comfort zone. My quiet denial. The emotional holding pattern I couldn't break out of.

But the thing about maybe is that it doesn't protect you—it preserves the pain. It keeps the wound open just enough so that you never heal.

I didn't want to ask him. Because as long as I didn't, the answer could still be maybe. And sometimes, maybe is the only thing that keeps you going.

But I finally asked. I asked him how he felt about me. If there was any chance. Any at all.

And I got my answer. No.

He asked me to let go.

And with that, I had to. Not just of him—but of the hope. The story. The dream I'd kept alive far too long.

The Shattering

I've been broken before. But this time felt different.

This time, I didn't just lose love. I lost the last thread of hope I was holding on to. And that... that was the moment everything inside me shattered.

That was the moment I finally said goodbye. To him. To us. To the version of me who believed love alone could be enough.

I truly thought I could love him into loving me.

The Dangerous Place Called Maybe

There's something strangely powerful about maybe. It's not a promise. It's not a lie. It's just enough.

Maybe is where we go when the truth is too heavy to carry but we're not ready to put it down. It gives us something to hold when everything else is slipping away.

For a long time, maybe was my lifeline. Maybe he still loved me. Maybe he just needed time. Maybe I wasn't crazy to believe in us. Maybe if I loved harder. Maybe, if I held on just a little longer, things would change.

I didn't need guarantees. I just needed that one thin thread to keep me from falling apart.

And for a while, it worked. Maybe got me out of bed. Maybe helped me pretend I was strong—when I was vanishing.

But maybe is a dangerous place to live. Because the longer you stay there, the harder it becomes to come back to the truth.

And the truth was: He had already let go. Long before I did. Maybe even before I realized I was holding on.

Still, I clung to the fantasy. I replayed memories like a favorite song, searching for signs—proof that it wasn't one-sided.

Because to me, it mattered. Because to me, it was real. Because to me, that was unconditional love.

But maybe doesn't scream. It whispers. And I listened.

Even when my gut said I was waiting for something that wasn't coming. Even when my friends gently told me to move on. Even when the distance between us became undeniable.

Still, I stayed. For the maybe. Because maybe meant I didn't have to grieve yet.

Letting go of that hope felt like letting go of something sacred. And maybe I wasn't ready. Maybe I was still looking for closure in places it could never exist.

The Moment I Chose Truth

But here's what I've learned: Closure doesn't come from someone else. It comes from within.

It comes from the moment you decide that maybe isn't enough anymore. That your love deserves to be returned. That your hope deserves peace.

And when that moment finally came, it was quiet. No fireworks. No dramatic goodbye.

Just a breath. A whisper to myself: *"You need to let him go. You are done."*

And I was.

Done holding space for someone who no longer showed up. Done rewriting the story to protect myself from the truth. Done living in maybe.

Because maybe kept me alive. But the truth? The truth will set me free.

Eventually, even maybe began to feel heavy. It no longer soothed me. It started to haunt me.

Because when you live in maybe, you're not really living at all—you're waiting. You're stuck in a hallway between what was and what will never be, replaying echoes and mistaking them for doors.

I kept hoping F. would return, but in doing so, I kept abandoning myself.

And one day, I realized: If I had to hold my breath around someone, it wasn't love. If I had to shrink myself to be chosen, it wasn't love. If I had to wait to be worthy, it was never love.

It was fantasy. Longing. Projection. Attachment. But not love—not the kind that stays.

The truth was already inside me. I just had to be brave enough to stop covering it up with false hope. I had to stop confusing crumbs for a feast. I had to stop calling my own starvation romance.

So I began to loosen my grip. Not all at once. Not easily. But with each breath, each boundary, each moment of clarity, I chose to stop living in maybe.

Because I finally understood: *"Maybe"* is where love quietly withers. *Truth is where I rise.* And I am rising now.

✦ ✦ ✦

"Maybe kept me waiting in the dark. Truth
is what walked me into the light."

Chapter 3

How It All Started — The Beginning of an End

"Some beginnings are just endings in disguise—
soft openings to stories that were never meant
to last, but still meant to change us."

It was New Year's Eve—the first one after COVID—when life finally began to feel somewhat normal again. People were coming out of their homes, reconnecting, celebrating, and pretending that the world hadn't just shifted beneath our feet.

It was a time of cautious hope and tentative joy. And what better moment to start something new than the beginning of a new year—surrounded by laughter, resolutions, and the clink of champagne glasses?

I was at my friend Keith's apartment that night, surrounded by familiar faces, trying to have a good time in New York City. But something inside me felt off. I was there physically, but my mind was scattered, wandering anywhere but the room I stood in.

Disconnected. Bored. Numb.

I couldn't explain the feeling—I just knew I didn't want to be there. I wanted more. Something different. Something alive.

So I texted my friend Ian—well-known in the city for throwing wild parties—and asked if anything was happening. Officially, the city was still half-closed. Large gatherings weren't allowed, but the underground scene had found ways around it.

Of course, there were secret parties that night. And he invited me to one.

Without much hesitation, I walked over to Keith, hugged him, and apologized. *"I'm sorry, but I have to go,"* I said. And I left.

I felt a little guilty leaving everyone behind, but something in me needed to go. I didn't know why—I just knew I had to follow that urge.

I went to Ian's place to get ready, and before long, I was thrown into a car with strangers, heading to Brooklyn. But by the time we arrived, the party had already been shut down—cops had been called. For a moment, we had nowhere to go.

But the night wasn't over.

Ian decided to host the party at his apartment, so we all migrated there—spilling back into Manhattan like a wave of champagne and glitter.

The moment we stepped inside, it felt like stepping into another world.

Music pulsed through the walls—the kind that made your body move before you even realized it. The living room was a kaleidoscope of color—fairy lights draped across windows, half-empty glasses on every surface, people swaying and laughing like the night could never end.

The energy was infectious. Conversations overlapped, voices rising above the beat, bursts of laughter ringing out like fireworks. Someone was dancing in the kitchen with a bottle of prosecco, while others perched on the couch, lost in deep conversations that only happen when the clock has long passed midnight.

On the coffee table, between scattered bottles, were small, tell-tale lines of white powder, crumpled bills, and the quiet exchange of knowing glances.

I let myself get pulled into it all—dancing until my feet ached, my cheeks warm from smiling, my voice hoarse from singing along to songs I barely knew. It was fun—maybe a little too much fun—but for once, I didn't care.

I let myself disappear into the blur of it, into the haze that made the night feel endless. Hours slipped by like water in my hands, the windows slowly shifting from black night to a pale blue glow.

By the time I finally checked the time, it was 8 a.m. on New Year's Day. My body was still buzzing from the music, the laughter, and the haze of it all, but I knew it was time to go home and let the city rest—and maybe, finally, so would I.

But once I got home—showered and in bed—I couldn't sleep. My body was exhausted, but my mind was wide awake. Restless.

After tossing and turning for an hour, I made a decision: I was going back to the party.

And that's when I saw him.

F.

Confident. Charismatic. Effortlessly magnetic.

He wasn't like anyone I'd ever met. He had this presence—like he didn't have to try to be noticed. He just was.

Tall, with dark hair that fell in a way that looked accidental yet perfect, catching the light like it had secrets to keep. A boyish, yet undeniably masculine face—soft edges concealing a quiet strength.

Eyes dark, endless, and piercing, as if they weren't just looking at you, but through you. They didn't wander. They locked. And when they did, the rest of the world disappeared.

His smile was magnetic—not just beautiful, but dangerous. The kind that made you forget where you were, what you were saying, even who you thought you were.

His skin held the warmth of sunlight, as if he carried summer with him no matter the season. Broad, strong shoulders that made you feel small in the best possible way. Hands that looked like they'd know exactly how to hold you—steady, sure, unshakable.

And a way of moving, of carrying himself, that told you he belonged anywhere he walked into—without ever needing to prove it.

I couldn't stop looking at him. I was drawn in instantly, like gravity. His smile, his energy, the way he carried himself—it was captivating.

I was mesmerized. Obsessed, even.

I watched him laugh with his friends, fully immersed in the moment, completely unaware of me. Or so I thought.

I tried to get closer, hoping he'd see me. But with my shyness, there was no way I'd start a conversation. So I drifted, talked to others, tried to blend in.

Eventually, I found myself talking to someone I didn't know—Andrew. We chatted, drank champagne, danced. There was music, movement, energy. And then, we kissed.

In that exact moment, F appeared.

He gently pushed Andrew aside and said, with a quiet authority: *"I saw him first."*

I was stunned. I thought he hadn't noticed me at all. But he had.

And that... was the moment it all began.

We started talking—just a simple conversation. But it didn't feel simple.

It felt like the universe had been holding its breath, waiting for this exact moment to release us into each other's orbit.

The room was alive—laughter spilling from every corner, music pulsing through the floorboards, champagne glasses clinking like tiny bells—but all of it blurred into background noise. The world stepped back, as if it knew this wasn't about anyone else.

His eyes found mine and didn't let go. They held me there, steady, unhurried, like he wasn't just looking at me but through me—past the masks, past the stories I rehearsed for strangers, into the places I swore I'd never show anyone.

And something inside me shifted. Quietly. Inevitably. Like the ground had tilted beneath me, and suddenly gravity itself had changed.

We danced. The bass pounded in my chest, but the rhythm we moved to was something different—something only we could hear. His laugh tumbled into mine, reckless and light, and for a breathless stretch of time it felt like we had been laughing together our whole lives.

We drifted between the noise and the silence, the crowd and the spaces that felt like ours alone. Stolen glances became confessions. Small touches became promises.

We stayed awake until the night surrendered to morning. Hours vanished like smoke.

We talked about everything and nothing—about dreams, about regrets, about the kind of thoughts you usually swallow but somehow trusted to say aloud in the dark.

I remember the cool slip of a champagne glass from my fingers, the golden blur of streetlights through the window, the soft blue edge of dawn pressing against the horizon. The world was forgiving in that light, as if it was blessing what it saw.

And somewhere between the last sip of the night and the first light of the year, I fell.

I don't know if I fell for him, or for the idea of him—the dream my heart had been aching to believe in. The way he made me feel less like a stranger in my own skin. The way he slowed the world down and made space for something I had almost stopped believing in.

But even in the beauty of it, something in me knew.

Moments like this don't last. They live in the spaces between what is real and what we wish could be.

He was never mine—not truly. Maybe he wasn't meant to be.

And maybe that's why it felt like magic. Because it was borrowed time. Because it was fleeting. Because love—at least the kind that catches you off guard—is always just a heartbeat away from slipping through your fingers.

Some beginnings are really just borrowed time disguised as magic.

✦ ✦ ✦

"The beginning felt like a spark—but some fires are only meant to burn long enough to leave you changed."

Chapter 4

The First Yes

*"The first yes is never just about a moment—it's the doorway
to everything your heart secretly hoped was possible."*

Before I left the party, we exchanged Instagrams and numbers. He didn't want me to go—I could feel it in the way his gaze lingered, in the almost-question caught in the curve of his smile. And truthfully, I didn't want to leave either. But I had already made plans with two of my friends for the day, and I didn't want to cancel at the last minute.

It was our tradition—our annual trip to a little shop in the Lower East Side of Manhattan called Enchantments. Every New Year's Day, the three of us would go there to get our intention candles for the year ahead. You'd tell the "witch" behind the counter your hopes, your goals, your heart's quiet wishes for the next twelve months, and she would carve a candle just for you—blessing it with ancient herbs and oils, sealing your words in wax. The idea was to burn it all the way down, usually over three days, until your intention found its way into reality.

Whether it worked or not, I couldn't say. But it was ours—our little ritual that felt like magic, even if it was just the kind we created for ourselves. And as I walked away that day, I couldn't shake the feeling that maybe I was leaving something else behind too—something that might not wait for me to come back. Still, I promised I would text him. And I did.

I wanted to message him the moment I got home. My fingers hovered over my phone all night, but I held back. I've always had this habit of giving too much, too soon—of loving with a whole, open heart before the other person has even unwrapped their own. This time, I told myself, I'd be strong. I'd hold the urge.

So I waited until the next day.

Still, I couldn't stop thinking about him—the way he'd looked at me when I said I had to go. Like he was trying to memorize me, just in case. That expression stayed with me, looping in my mind until I gave in and opened Instagram. I scrolled through his profile as if I were tracing the edges of a photograph. Every picture was a little piece of him—smiles, friends, travels—but none of them looked quite like the version I'd met that night. That version felt more... ours.

Finally, I picked up my phone and typed: *"Hey, made it to my candle ritual. I'll tell you if I magically get everything I wished for."*

It didn't take long. Three dots appeared. *"You should've wished to stay with me longer."*

I smiled, biting my lip. *"Maybe I did."*

There was a pause, then: *"I'm free tomorrow night. You?"*

And just like that, we made a plan to meet the following day. I invited him over—COVID was still lingering, and most places were closed. So it would just be us.

The next day moved painfully slow, each hour stretching out as if the universe was testing my patience. By late afternoon, I stood in front of my closet, staring at my clothes like they might hold the answer. I didn't want to look like I was trying too hard, but I wanted him to notice. I wanted him to look at me the way he had at the party—like I was the only thing in the room worth paying attention to.

I settled on something simple, soft against my skin, the kind of outfit that whispered instead of shouted. I left my hair slightly undone, a little wild—like maybe I'd just come from somewhere else, but had ended up here, with him, on purpose.

I spent the whole day preparing. I cleaned my apartment as if it were about to be featured in a magazine. I ran to the store for wine, snacks, candles—anything that could make the evening feel like something. I was nervous, happy, excited, and overwhelmed. I felt like a teenager again, and I loved it.

His smile—God, that smile. Just the thought of it made my heart race and my cheeks lift. It wasn't just charming—it was honest. Like he wasn't trying to impress anyone. Like he had nothing to prove. That smile melted me every time, and I couldn't wait to see it again.

When the doorbell finally rang, I froze for a second. *"This is it,"* I thought.

The knock was softer than I expected—like he didn't want to startle me, like he already belonged here.

I opened the door, and for a moment, we just stood there. He on the threshold, me holding the edge of the door, both of us caught in that quiet second where time forgets to move. He was wearing a simple white sweater, but somehow it felt like the most perfect thing he could have chosen. His hair was a little messy, like he'd run his hands through it on the way over.

"Hey," he said, and it wasn't just a greeting. It was an unspoken *"I'm here."*

I stepped aside to let him in, and as he passed me, I caught the faintest trace of his cologne—warm, subtle, the kind that lingers just enough to make you lean in again. He glanced around the candlelit room, then back at me, and there was something in his eyes I couldn't name yet.

It wasn't the start of the night—it was the start of something.

He hugged me—big, warm, familiar—and then kissed me, soft and slow. In that moment, I was in heaven. Nothing else mattered.

He set his phone and keys on the counter like he'd been here before, like my place was already familiar to him. I offered him a drink, more to give my hands something to do than because I thought he was thirsty.

We sat on the couch, a careful distance between us at first—the kind that says *I don't want to rush this, but I want to be closer.* The flicker of candlelight softened the edges of everything, casting his face in a warm glow that made it hard to focus on anything he was saying. I caught myself staring at the curve of his jaw, the way his lips moved when he spoke, the quiet steadiness in his voice.

We talked about nothing and everything—movies, music, travel—
each topic an excuse to stay in the moment. Every so often, his knee
would brush against mine, and each time it felt deliberate. I could feel
the space between us shrinking, not because we moved, but because
the air itself seemed to draw us closer.

At one point, I laughed at something he said, and when I looked
up, his eyes were already on me. Not a quick glance—he was looking.
Holding me there. And in that moment, it felt like the rest of the night
had already been decided, even if neither of us had said a word.

We talked for hours. I wanted to know everything—who he was,
where he'd been, why we hadn't met sooner. But maybe the timing had to be exactly right. Maybe we wouldn't have seen each other
before that New Year's Eve, even if we'd been standing side by side.

He told me about his life, his past, and growing up in Colombia. I
shared my story, the version of me I usually keep hidden until someone
earns it. But with him, it just came out—natural, easy. We laughed.
We drank wine. We listened. We saw each other.

It felt perfect.

Eventually, we curled up to watch *Veneno*, a Spanish series he
loved. It had English subtitles, but to be honest, I didn't follow much
of the story. I couldn't stop looking at him—his face, his expressions,
the way he shifted when he got excited or thoughtful. I was captivated.

The conversation slowed, not because we'd run out of things to
say, but because words started to feel unnecessary. There was a different kind of language building between us—one made of glances,
pauses, and the quiet hum of being so aware of someone that you
could almost hear their heartbeat.

He leaned back slightly, his arm resting along the back of the
couch, his fingers brushing the top of my shoulder. It was the lightest
touch, but it set something in motion. I turned toward him, and the
space between us—small as it already was—suddenly felt like the only
thing in the world worth crossing.

His eyes searched mine, as if he was giving me time to look away.
I didn't. I couldn't.

And then he leaned in—slow, unhurried, like he wanted to make
sure I'd remember every fraction of a second before our lips touched.

When they finally did, it wasn't rushed or desperate. It was steady, certain—like we'd both been waiting for it without realizing how much until right now. His hand found the side of my face, warm and sure, and I felt myself lean into it like it was the most natural thing in the world.

The candlelight flickered against the walls, shadows dancing around us, and for that moment, there was no pandemic, no outside world—just him, and the quiet, undeniable pull that had brought him here.

Outside, New York was still roaring—sirens slicing through the night, taxis blaring their horns, footsteps echoing on wet pavement. The city never stopped for anyone. But here, in my small apartment, time had bent. The noise couldn't reach us. The rush couldn't touch us. The world was still spinning out there, but with him, it felt like it had paused—just long enough for me to memorize the way his hand felt against my face, the way his eyes anchored me, the way the city could keep moving forever, and I wouldn't notice, not while he was here.

And then we started to cuddle.

When he held me, the world went still. Time slowed down. It was like nothing else existed outside that moment. I had never felt that kind of peace before. That kind of safe. He made me feel seen, protected, understood… and wanted. And with that quiet confidence, that mix of sweetness and edge—that bad boy spark—he completely disarmed me.

One thing led to another, and soon we found ourselves in my bedroom. More connected than before. More vulnerable. More open.

And for the first time in my life, I felt like I was making love—not just having sex.

His touch was electric. His breath, his lips, the way he moved, the way he looked at me—it was euphoria. It was magic. It was everything.

I will never forget that night. Not because of what happened—but because of how it happened. The way I surrendered. The way I let go. The way I let someone all the way in.

And I don't let people in…

I opened my heart to him that night. Fully. Recklessly. Unconditionally.

And deep down, a quiet voice whispered: *"Be careful… you're falling fast."*

But I didn't listen. Because in that moment—I didn't want to be careful. I just wanted him.

That night, I didn't just let him in — I let myself be seen

✦   ✦   ✦

*"Some hearts aren't taken—they're offered, fully
and fearlessly, in moments that feel like forever…
even when forever never promised to stay."*

Chapter 5

The Goodbye That Came Too Soon

"Sometimes love begins like a whisper and ends like an echo—fading before you ever had the chance to hold it fully."

But my happiness didn't last long.

We were still on the couch, the city long forgotten. The candles had burned low, their wax pooling at the edges. We were tangled together under the blanket—skin warm against skin, my head resting against his chest, listening to the slow, steady rhythm of his breathing.

The quiet between us wasn't awkward—it was full, the kind of silence that feels like it belongs.

I was bare beneath the blanket, my legs curled against his, my fingers tracing absent patterns along his arm. Outside, New York's night was still restless—horns, sirens, voices—but in here, it was just us.

And then, softly, almost like he didn't want to disturb the stillness, he said: *"I'm moving to Orlando."*

I froze. For a second, I thought I'd misheard him. "Orlando?" I lifted my head, searching his face for some sign that it was a joke, that maybe I'd misunderstood. But he was serious—too serious.

"In a few days," he added, like it was nothing.

The blanket suddenly felt too thin. The room too small. I stared at him, trying to process the words—*leaving, a few days, gone*—but they just hung in the air, heavy and impossible. My chest tightened, and even though we were still wrapped around each other, I felt an ache like he was already gone.

He explained it gently. New York hadn't been easy since COVID. Jobs were scarce. Rent was high. Life was still crawling back to normal, and survival sometimes meant sacrifice. A friend in Orlando managed a restaurant and had offered him a job as a bartender.

It wasn't permanent, he said. Just temporary. Just until things got better. He'd be back in April, when the city thawed, when opportunities returned with the spring.

I nodded. I understood. I really did. But understanding didn't stop my heart from breaking.

"We just met. I just found you. And now you're leaving?"

I couldn't make sense of the pain I was feeling for someone I had just begun to know. But something about him had already imprinted on me—so deeply, so completely. I didn't want to lose him. I couldn't.

We talked it through—quietly, intimately, still wrapped in blankets and promises we hadn't tested yet.

"I don't want this to be over," I said, my voice barely above a whisper. My fingers traced circles on the back of his hand, like maybe if I kept touching him, he couldn't leave.

His eyes softened. *"It doesn't have to be."* He shifted closer, the blanket falling slightly off his shoulder. *"We can try. Long distance. Phone calls. Visits."*

"I'll fly to Orlando," I said instantly, like the words had been waiting in my chest all along.

His lips curved into a half-smile. *"And I can come back here. I still have friends in the city…"* His gaze held mine for a beat longer. *"…and you."*

I swallowed hard. *"We can make it work."*

"We will make it work," he said, with the kind of certainty I wanted to believe in. His thumb brushed over my knuckles, slow and deliberate, like a quiet promise.

Silence settled between us, not heavy, but tender—an understanding that neither of us wanted to name out loud. Outside, the city roared on without us, but here, in this small cocoon of candlelight and warmth, we made our own version of the future.

There was no other option in my mind. I wasn't ready to let go of something that had only just begun. I wasn't ready to say goodbye to the person who, somehow, already felt like home.

Yes, I know what people might think—it was too soon, too fast, too much. But the truth is, I loved him. Even then. Even after only a few days. Even now.

Even though our story didn't last the way I hoped it would… he is, and always will be, the love of my life.

I still love him.

And no, that love didn't disappear when things ended. Real love doesn't vanish. It settles in your bones. It lives quietly in the background of your days. It reminds you of the way your heart once opened without fear.

"Some goodbyes don't wait for the right time. They arrive too soon, too sharp, and all you can do is hold on to the love that didn't get the chance to grow—but still somehow never left."

Chapter 6

Holding On Across the Distance

"Distance doesn't break a bond—it only asks if it was real enough to survive the stretch."

A few days later, the moment I had been dreading finally came—F was leaving for Orlando.

I didn't see him that day. I couldn't. The thought of saying goodbye felt unbearable. How do you let go of someone you love with your entire heart? How do you look them in the eyes, knowing it might be the last time? I wasn't ready.

Maybe I never would be.

It all felt too fast. Too unfair. We had just found each other—and now I was losing him. And yet, despite everything, I was determined to stay connected. To fight for this, no matter the distance. I didn't know how he felt anymore, but I was certain of how I felt about him. From the very beginning, I knew my heart belonged to him.

He texted me when he arrived in Orlando. He wasn't happy. He missed his friends, his routine, his familiarity. He had left behind the world he knew—again. Just like he had once left Colombia for New York, chasing a better life, something more aligned with who he wanted to be.

I understood that feeling more than anyone.

I had done it too—left everything I knew in Poland at nineteen and moved across the ocean with nothing but a dream and a suitcase full of fear. I knew what it meant to start over. I knew the cost of change.

Sometimes we have to let go of one life to build another. One that feels more like home. One that lets us be who we truly are.

So I didn't pressure him. I didn't demand anything from him. I knew he was overwhelmed, scared, still trying to find his footing. Even if the move was temporary, it was still a rupture—a change big enough to shake everything.

Instead, I gave him space. And we stayed in touch.

We texted every day. We tried. We did our best to keep this fragile, beautiful thing we had found alive.

And even though miles separated us, he was with me constantly. I thought about him all the time—wondering if he was okay, if he was adjusting, if he missed me. I stared at the few pictures we had together like they were relics from another life. I looked at his smile and felt both warmth and longing.

I wondered what I meant to him now. If he still thought about me before falling asleep. If he remembered the little moments we shared. If he replayed our memories the way I did—on a loop, like a favorite movie I didn't want to end.

There were so many questions. So few answers.

But through all that uncertainty, I clung to one truth—I wasn't ready to let go.

I believed there was something worth saving, even if I couldn't see the shape of it anymore. I believed in us with the kind of stubborn hope that ignores reason, the kind that keeps you reaching for a hand that may never reach back.

I believed in the quiet moments we had built, in the unspoken bond that I swore still lived between us, even as time and distance tried to unravel it.

I believed in us, even when the world around us kept shifting, even when everything and everyone seemed to tell me it was over.

And then, as the days slipped by, a small spark of possibility emerged—we made a plan. I would visit him in Orlando.

Finally, I had something to hold on to. Something to look forward to.

The thought of seeing him again filled me with hope. I imagined his face when he saw me. That smile. That hug. The words I had been holding onto for weeks: *"I missed you. I love you. I'm still here."*

I counted the days.

Not just because I missed him—but because I needed to believe that love could survive the distance. That sometimes, what's meant to be doesn't fall apart—it just waits to be reunited.

"Some hearts don't say goodbye—they say, 'Wait for me.' And sometimes, love waits... just long enough to find its way back."

Chapter 7

Orlando – A Different Kind of Beginning

"Reunions are never just meetings—they are tests of the heart, asking if love can survive the spaces in between."

The days leading up to my trip to Orlando felt like slow motion—each hour stretching longer than the last. I was excited, yes. But underneath that excitement lived something quieter, heavier: fear.

I was terrified. Terrified of what it would feel like to see him again. Terrified of how my heart might betray me the second I saw his face. Terrified that this visit I had wrapped in hope might unravel into disappointment.

I wanted this trip to be a fresh start. A chance to reconnect. To rewrite the ending we were headed toward.

But I also knew—we couldn't go back. Not to the way things were. Too much had already happened. Too many silences. Too many questions. If we were going to try again, it had to be different this time. More honest. More careful. More real.

Still, my heart was soft for him.

I packed like I was preparing for both a reunion and a reckoning. Every choice felt deliberate, almost ceremonial. I folded the shirts I knew I felt good in—the black button-down that fit just right across my shoulders, the soft white T-shirt, and the dark jeans that somehow made me feel both confident and comfortable. I added a pair of grey linen shorts for the Florida heat, casual enough for the day but sharp enough to catch his attention.

And then there was the silver bracelet with two angel wings. The first time he saw it, we'd been at my apartment before he left New York. I was wearing it without thinking, and he reached for my wrist, tracing the wings with his thumb. *"I like this,"* he'd said, his voice soft, almost reverent.

So I found another one—identical to mine—and slipped it into my bag. It wasn't just a gift. It was a quiet message. A way of saying, *I'm with you, even when I'm not there.*

I replayed every version of how our first hug might feel. Would it be awkward? Would it feel like coming home? Would he pull away? Or would we fall into each other like no time had passed?

I boarded the plane with a stomach full of nerves and a suitcase full of hope.

As we landed, I stared out the window and whispered a quiet promise to myself: *"No matter how this goes, you will stay true to who you are. You will show up as yourself—and that will be enough."*

I checked into the hotel, the cool blast of air conditioning hitting my skin as I stepped into the quiet, neutral-toned room. I unpacked slowly, laying each shirt neatly in the drawer, placing the bracelet box carefully on the nightstand like it was too important to hide away.

In the shower, I let the hot water run over me until the travel fatigue melted away, steam curling around me like it was sealing me inside this long-awaited moment.

I took my time getting ready—shaving carefully, running my fingers through my hair until it fell just right, pulling on the fitted black T-shirt that hugged my shoulders and chest the way I knew he'd notice. I added a spritz of the cologne he once said he liked, the scent settling on my skin like a quiet promise.

By the time I stepped back and looked at myself in the mirror, I didn't just want to look good—I wanted to look like the version of me he'd remember. The one he'd want to hold onto.

He was still at work and wouldn't be able to meet me until later that evening. I had no idea what to do with myself during those hours. My body was in the room, but my heart was already with him.

I was ready. Ready to see him. Ready to kiss him. Ready to feel what it was like to be with him again.

As the hour drew closer, my heart beat faster. Every sound in the hallway made me turn my head. And then—finally—he arrived.

I spotted him in the hotel lobby before he saw me, and for a second, I just watched him walk toward me. He looked the same, but somehow different. Familiar, yet with a kind of distance I couldn't quite name. My heart reacted before my mind could catch up.

When he reached me, he wrapped me in a hug, and it was all there again—that ache, that tenderness, that desperate feeling of home. Then I saw his smile. The way his eyes lit up. And in that moment, I knew—he still had feelings for me. And just like that, mine deepened all over again.

We stepped into the elevator together, the hum of the machinery filling the silence. The space was small, our shoulders brushing with each slight movement. I could feel the warmth radiating off him, smell the faint trace of his cologne mingling with mine. Neither of us said much, but there was a pull between us—like every floor we passed was winding the cord tighter.

His hand brushed against mine once, maybe by accident, maybe not, and it sent a flicker of heat through me.

When the doors finally slid open, we walked down the hallway side by side, that invisible thread between us tugging just a little harder. The moment we stepped inside the room, we sank onto the couch together, curling into each other like no time had passed at all.

I was in heaven. To be next to him… to smell him… to feel his touch again—it was enough. More than enough.

He was gentle, just like he had been the first night he ever came over to my apartment. He made me feel seen. Wanted. Important. The way he looked at me, the way he held me, the way he rested his head on my chest—it felt like everything I had been longing for.

I wanted to stop time right there—to keep him exactly where he was, close enough that I could feel the steady rise and fall of his chest against mine.

We didn't go out that night. The city outside could have been on fire for all we knew; we stayed in, wrapped in the small, private world of the room. The TV flickered in front of us, casting shifting light across his face. Sometimes we watched, sometimes we forgot it was even on. He'd say something that made me laugh, and I'd watch the corner of his mouth curve in response—like my laughter had pulled something out of him he hadn't realized was still there.

At some point, he shifted, laying his head on my chest. My arms folded around him instinctively, holding him there. My face sank into his hair, breathing him in—his shampoo, faintly herbal, mixing with the warm, subtle trace of his cologne. It was a scent I could have memorized in one breath and recognized for the rest of my life.

Our legs tangled together on the couch, the blanket slipping down just enough for my skin to brush his. Every so often, his fingertips traced idle lines along my arm, sending a warmth through me that had nothing to do with the temperature in the room.

The air was quiet except for the low hum of the TV and the soft cadence of his voice.

There was no rush. No agenda. Just the weight of him against me, the sound of his breathing, the way his hair tickled my chin when he moved. It felt like the kind of night you only get once—so simple it's almost ordinary, until you realize you'd give anything to live it over and over again.

The minutes stretched and softened, the way they do when you're not watching the clock. His breathing grew slower, more even, like he was listening to my heartbeat and letting it set his pace. My hand rested on the back of his neck, my thumb moving in slow, absent circles, feeling the warmth of his skin beneath my touch.

The TV murmured in the background, the light flickering across the walls, but neither of us was really paying attention anymore. My focus narrowed to the weight of him against me, the subtle rise and fall with each breath, the way his hair brushed my jaw whenever he shifted.

Every inhale brought more of him into me—his scent, his warmth, the quiet safety that seemed to wrap itself around us like another blanket.

His arm was draped across my waist, his fingers curled lightly into my side, as if even in sleep he wasn't ready to let go. My own eyes began to grow heavy, and I found myself tracing the line of his shoulder with my fingertips, memorizing him in case the morning came too soon.

Outside, the city kept moving, impatient as ever. But in here, the night was ours. The world had shrunk to the slow rhythm of our breathing, the soft press of skin, the steady heartbeat that promised we were exactly where we were supposed to be.

And somewhere between one breath and the next, we drifted into sleep—still holding onto each other like we might never get another night like this.

Everything I had feared before the trip faded away. I was with the love of my life, and for that one night, everything felt right. It was perfect. At least, it was perfect in my eyes.

✦　✦　✦

"Sometimes the heart remembers before the
mind can catch up—and in one hug, everything
you tried to forget comes rushing back."

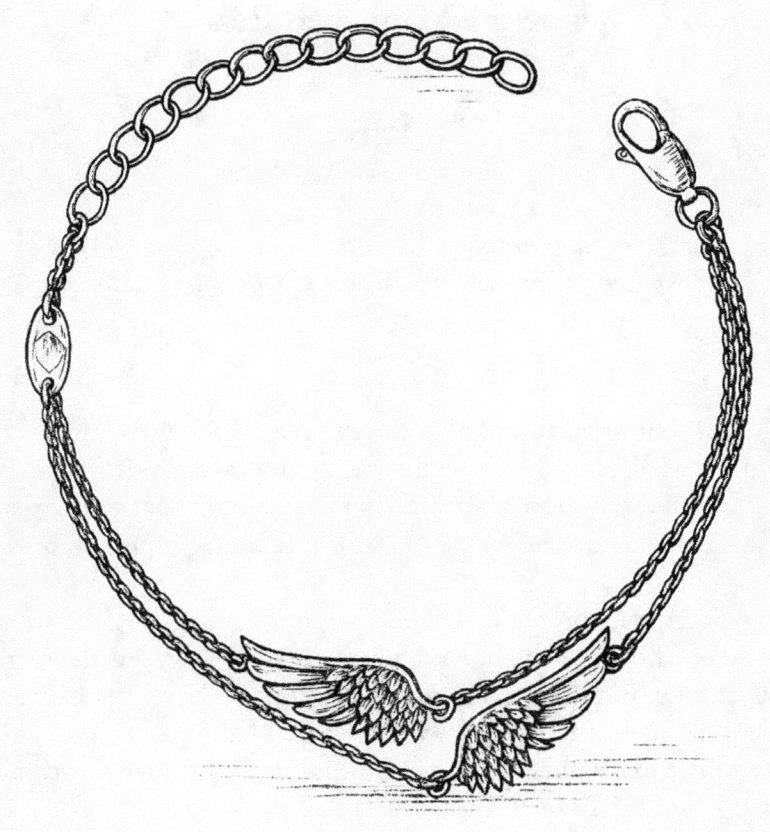

Chapter 8

Where the Magic Felt Real

"Sometimes the most ordinary days become extraordinary—not because of where you are, but because of who you're with."

The next morning, we woke up early to go to Disney World. But I was already there—living inside my own kind of Disney World, the kind you don't buy tickets for, the kind that only exists when someone makes the whole world feel like magic just by being in it.

I was still sitting on the bed when the door opened.

He stepped out slowly, like the universe knew I needed the extra seconds to take him in. The hallway light caught the edge of his face first—soft, golden, still touched with sleep. His hair was perfectly imperfect, a little messy, like he'd just run his hands through it without thinking. And then I saw it: the Snoopy t-shirt.

It wasn't just a shirt—it was him in a single frame. Easy. Playful. Unaware of how much it suited him. The cotton hung loose over his shoulders, faint wrinkles catching the morning light like little lines in a photograph you want to keep forever. He tugged at the hem absently, glancing down for half a second, and in that moment he wasn't just the man I had been falling for—he was a boy again. The one with the mischievous spark in his eyes, the one who made you forget the world was heavy.

And those eyes... God, those eyes. They met mine and held me there, like they'd been waiting all morning to find me. My chest tightened, my breath stilled, and my heart... my heart just went. That dizzy, weightless kind of falling where you're not sure if you're flying or plummeting, only that you couldn't stop even if you tried.

From that day forward, Snoopy became our symbol. Every time I saw that little cartoon dog, I saw him. And every time I thought of him, I smiled—because it reminded me that somehow, this stranger I had only just met had become the most important person in my life.

When we arrived at Disneyland, masks were still required because of COVID. He pulled one on with a Mickey Mouse print, and I couldn't help but laugh softly under my breath—it was almost too perfect. The Snoopy shirt, the Mickey mask, those eyes still glinting with that same quiet mischief. It felt like the whole day had been drawn up in some secret corner of the universe just for us.

As we walked through the gates, the smell of popcorn and the faint sound of distant music wrapped around us. Every so often, I'd glance at him, and each time I did, I fell in love all over again—quietly, without fanfare, in the way you fall when you're already too far gone. And in that moment, surrounded by strangers, laughter, and the hum of magic in the air, I told myself to remember everything—the way his hand brushed mine, the way his eyes crinkled when he smiled, the way the sunlight hit his face—because part of me was afraid this was the kind of day you only get once.

From the moment we stepped into the park, it was like the world had been repainted in brighter colors. We laughed at nothing and everything. We explored every corner of the park like kids set loose—no agenda except to see, taste, and feel it all.

We tried warm pretzels dusted with salt, Dole Whip that melted faster than we could eat it. We shared a dripping ice cream cone, passing it back and forth until it was nothing but a sticky napkin and two smiling mouths. Every ride, every stall, every hidden corner felt like its own little adventure.

He held my hand as we walked, his thumb brushing over my skin like it was second nature. And every time we paused to take in the view or catch our breath, he'd glance at me with that same soft, steady expression—like I was the best part of the day for him.

He checked on me often—"You okay?"—and each time, I felt that quiet swell in my chest. He hugged me in the middle of the crowd, pulling me in close as if we were the only two people there. And the way he looked at me… it was the kind of look you can't fake. Gentle. Present. Full of something I didn't want to name too soon, but felt in every bone in my body.

I didn't want that day to end. But I knew it would. The next morning, he'd go back to work. I'd return to New York. The magic would spill back into everyday life—the hustle, the distance, the questions. But that day, we still had each other. And for that moment, that was all that mattered.

Just before we left the park, he asked me to wait outside while he ran into the souvenir store. I watched him weave through the crowd, disappearing into a sea of families and balloons. When he came back, he had something tucked behind his back and a smile that made my heart skip a beat.

Then he revealed it—a coffee mug shaped like Simba from *The Lion King*.

The movie we had watched the night before. The one I had told him was my favorite.

It wasn't just a gift—it was everything, proof he'd been listening. Proof that he noticed the small things. And that simple gesture, that remembering, was enough to make me fall for him all over again.

He made me so happy that day. Happier than I had felt in a long, long time. It wasn't the loud, dizzy kind of happiness that burns too bright and too fast—it was the quiet, steady kind that sinks into you, fills all the empty corners, and makes you feel like maybe you've finally found somewhere to rest.

Every laugh we shared loosened something in me I didn't even realize I'd been holding. Every time his fingers tightened gently around mine, I felt grounded, like I was exactly where I was supposed to be.

As we walked together, my hand in his, I found myself wondering quietly… *Do I make him this happy too?*

The thought lodged itself in my chest and stayed there. He wasn't very expressive when it came to talking about feelings. He never said much—not in words, anyway. But he showed it in other ways: the way he slowed his pace to match mine, the way he looked at me when he thought I wasn't paying attention, the way he kept checking that I was warm enough, comfortable enough, okay enough. Little things that didn't ask for attention but carried meaning all the same.

I figured that maybe that was just who he was. Not everyone speaks in declarations. Some people speak in presence—in showing up, in remembering, in reaching for your hand without thinking. And somehow, that meant more to me than any perfectly chosen words ever could.

That mystery—the parts of him I hadn't unlocked yet—only drew me in further. It made me want to learn every shade of him, every unspoken thought, every reason behind the way he was.

And as the day went on, I felt this ache—not a painful one, but the kind that comes from knowing you've stumbled into something rare. I didn't want the moment to end. I didn't want us to end.

All I wanted… was more.

More time. More smiles. More of him.

And for the first time in a long time, *more* didn't feel like a dangerous thing to want—it felt like hope.

✦　✦　✦

"Some days don't just pass—they imprint. And some people don't just visit your life—they become part of your favorite memory."

Chapter 9

Magic Continued

*"We're all searching for magic—but for one night, I
wasn't searching anymore. I had already found mine."*

I wanted to hold on to the magic for as long as I could. I wasn't ready
for the day to end. Not yet.

It had been one of those rare days when happiness felt pure—unshaken, almost childlike. For once, I could say it out loud without
hesitation: *I am happy.* And I truly was.

There was something about him I couldn't name, but it kept pulling me in. Just standing beside him filled me with a joy that doesn't
come often in life—the kind that feels borrowed from another world.

We were exhausted after a full day at the parks—our feet aching,
our bodies heavy from the miles we had walked, the rides we had
stood in line for, the endless swirl of colors and music still echoing in
our heads. But somehow, the tiredness didn't weigh us down. It only
wrapped around us like a soft blanket, the kind that makes you feel
safe rather than worn out.

Neither of us wanted to let go. The day had been too beautiful,
too rare, too full of something I didn't want to admit was already
slipping into memory. We weren't ready for the spell to break. The
world outside of this day felt too far away, too cold compared to the
warmth we were carrying between us.

So instead of retreating back to rest, we chose to chase it—to squeeze out every last drop of wonder. We walked hand in hand toward Disney Springs, that glowing mix of stores, lights, music, and laughter, where the night still shimmered with promise. It wasn't the same kind of magic as the parks, but it carried its own kind—quieter, softer, the afterglow of a day that still refused to die.

Everywhere we turned, there were families, couples, children—each chasing their own version of joy, their own piece of something to hold onto. And yet, for me, none of it mattered. My eyes didn't catch on the crowds or the stores or the lights strung up like stars. My eyes stayed on him.

Because the real magic wasn't in Disney. It was in the way his hand held mine. The way he laughed when something small caught his attention. The way just being beside him made me forget that the rest of the world even existed.

We weren't just strolling through shops. We were holding onto a dream neither of us was ready to wake up from.

The stores themselves felt like extensions of the parks, each one bursting with colors and familiar characters. We walked hand in hand, stopping to try on goofy hats, slipping into sweatshirts with oversized Mickey and Minnie across the chest, laughing at and with each other. Every little thing became funny, became sweet, became ours. For those moments, life felt weightless.

We touched everything like children who had wandered into a toy chest too big to ever empty—plush toys, mugs, keychains, all stamped with faces that reminded us of simpler times. Just being there with him, surrounded by the noise and light, I felt something inside me unclench. I wasn't worried about tomorrow, about what came after. I was just there—with him, in it, alive.

And then we stumbled into the Christmas section.

It stopped me in my tracks. The glow of twinkling lights, the smell of cinnamon candles burning nearby, the rows of ornaments hanging like tiny treasures—it was overwhelming in the best possible way. Christmas had always been my season, the one time of year I believed in everything good, no matter how broken life felt the rest of the time. Standing there with him, surrounded by so much joy, it felt like the universe had layered magic on top of magic, just for me.

My chest ached in the best way. I thought, *this is what happiness looks like, this is what it feels like when hope doesn't hurt.*

That's when I saw it. A Mickey Mouse ornament, small and simple, yet it called to me the way his smile did earlier that day when he slipped on that Mickey mask in the park. It wasn't just cute—it felt like a sign, like something I needed to hold onto. I picked it up, ran my fingers across its smooth surface, and I knew I had to have it.

As the cashier wrapped it in tissue paper, I drifted into a dream. I imagined us years from now, unpacking boxes of decorations, pulling out this ornament together. I imagined us stringing lights on a tree, laughing about how silly it was that our first Christmas memory together came from Disney. I knew I was running too far ahead, building a story out of thin air, but I couldn't stop. My heart wanted it so badly.

I pulled myself back, told myself to slow down, to let the magic unfold at its own pace. But still, I tucked the ornament close as if it could keep my secret wish safe.

Eventually hunger pulled us out of the store. We wandered until we landed at Planet Hollywood, almost by accident. Out of all the choices, we chose that one—and somehow it felt right, as if the night itself was guiding us.

The place was crowded, buzzing with tourists searching for their own piece of wonder. The restaurant was full of people searching for their own magic. And that's the truth—we all crave it. Even if it only lasts a night.

I looked around and thought: *That's what we're all doing, isn't it? Chasing magic. Needing it. Even if it only lasts a moment.*

But I wasn't searching anymore. I had already found mine. And I wanted it to last forever. Even if forever was never meant for us.

Still, I held on.

We slid into our booth, tired and hungry, but smiling like two kids who had stayed at the fair too long and didn't regret it. I barely glanced at the menu—the food didn't matter. He was beside me, and that was enough.

While we waited for our order, a woman with a camera appeared at our table. *"Would you like a picture?"* she asked, her voice bright, rehearsed from saying it a thousand times to couples before us.

We didn't even hesitate. *"Yes,"* we both said, almost in unison.

She snapped one photo, and then asked if she could take another— *"This time, maybe a kiss?"*

We looked at each other, almost shy, almost caught off guard, but then we leaned in.

And in that instant, the world disappeared.

His lips met mine, soft and sure, and the magic deepened. It wasn't just a kiss—it was an anchor. It was us suspended in a bubble no one else could touch. The restaurant noise fell away. The chaos, the exhaustion, the crowd—all of it blurred. All that existed was him and me.

When I saw the photo, something inside me stilled. It wasn't just a picture—it was proof. Proof that for a heartbeat in time, we were real. That I hadn't imagined it. That I hadn't dreamed him into my life only to wake up alone.

I didn't know then how much I would cling to that photo. How it would outlast the nights, the words, the silences. How it would become the only picture I couldn't bring myself to delete.

Because it wasn't just an image. It was a memory I could hold in my hands. A love that lived, even if it didn't last.

That photo carried everything—the joy, the hope, the belief, the magic.

That kiss wasn't just a kiss—it was an anchor. Proof that for a heartbeat in time, we were real. And even after the magic was gone, the picture remained. A reminder that once, for a fleeting moment, I had it all. And maybe that was the cruelest kind of magic—the kind that shows you forever in a single night, then leaves you holding only a photograph.

✦ ✦ ✦

"The picture became the only one I could never delete, because it wasn't just a memory. It was a love that lived, even if it didn't last."

Chapter 10

After the Magic

"The hardest goodbyes are the ones wrapped in silence—the kind where no one says the words, but you feel them anyway."

The morning I left Orlando, everything felt too quiet. The kind of quiet that makes you aware of your own breathing. The hotel room, once filled with laughter and whispered promises, now felt hollow—like the air itself had changed. My suitcase lay open on the floor, half-packed, clothes folded carelessly as if order no longer mattered. My heart felt the same—messy, unfinished, not ready to be closed.

I moved slowly, deliberately, pretending that if I took long enough, time might hesitate with me. I didn't want to go. I didn't want the magic to end, to watch it dissolve into just another memory. The morning light crept through the curtains in thin, faded strips, and even the sun felt muted, as if it knew this was the last day.

We didn't talk much. Maybe because we didn't know what to say. Maybe because the words would have felt too final. He sat on the edge of the bed, scrolling through his phone, and I busied myself with zippers and toiletries, both of us pretending to be occupied when really, we were just avoiding the truth. We both knew this was goodbye—but neither of us knew what kind. Was it temporary? Was it the last time? Were we walking away from something fragile but alive, or holding on to something that had already slipped through our fingers?

When it was finally time, we moved through the motions like actors in a scene we hadn't rehearsed. He walked me downstairs, the soft thud of our footsteps echoing in the hallway. Outside, the air was warm but carried a faint breeze, the kind that brushes past you without asking permission. My ride was already waiting, engine humming, a quiet reminder that this moment couldn't last.

We stood there for a second too long, the kind of pause that feels both heavy and fragile. His arms wrapped around me, and I let myself sink into it, memorizing the shape of him, the way his heartbeat felt against mine. I breathed him in, as if that could make it last longer, as if I could carry it with me once I was gone.

Neither of us said the words we were thinking. We didn't promise to see each other soon. We didn't say this was the end. We just held on until we couldn't anymore, and when I finally stepped into the car, I looked back to see him still standing there—hands in his pockets, head tilted slightly, watching me leave. I smiled through the ache in my chest, wondering if he knew I was already replaying the moment in my mind, just to keep it alive a little longer.

Just like that, the magic was over.

Back in New York, everything felt different. The city hadn't changed—but I had. The streets looked the same, the buildings stood still, but I didn't feel like the same person who had left a few days earlier. Something in me had softened and broken at the same time.

I missed him instantly.

His quiet smile. The way he rested his head on my chest. The little gestures that said *I see you*, even if the words never did.

At first, we kept our promises. The calls came regularly, the texts felt easy, and the distance—though heavy—seemed manageable. I told myself this was just a phase, that we'd find our rhythm again. But slowly, almost without noticing, the space between our words began to stretch. A day would pass without hearing from him, then two. Our conversations, once full of stories and laughter, became shorter, lighter—more polite than passionate.

And for a while, we tried. We stayed in touch—texts, calls, little check-ins that felt like lifelines. He even came back to New York a few times—not for me, but for his friends. And when it was convenient, we saw each other. I told myself it didn't matter why he was here, only that he was. I tried to focus on the fact that I still got to see him, to hear his voice in person, to feel that familiar pull when we were in the same room. But beneath the surface, it hurt—knowing I wasn't the reason he booked the flight, that I was more of an afterthought than a destination.

I wanted to believe our connection was strong enough to survive the distance, but every time he left again, I felt the quiet reminder that I wasn't the center of his world. And still, I clung to the moments we had, because letting them go felt impossible.

I started overanalyzing his replies—reading too much into the pauses, the periods, the questions he didn't answer. And when he came back to New York, it was less and less often. Even then, I wasn't always part of his plans right away. Sometimes I only saw him because I reached out first. Sometimes it felt like I was slotting myself into whatever free time was left after everyone else.

Each visit was shorter. More distant. Less magic.

I told myself that still counted for something. That maybe he was trying in his own way. That maybe his version of effort just looked different. And part of me genuinely believed that—because I could feel his care in small moments. But another part of me couldn't shake the truth: the more I tried, the more I poured in, the more I reached out and made space and showed up—the more he seemed to pull away.

And I couldn't understand why.

Why was love so hard for him? Why did he run every time I got closer? Why did it feel like the more I wanted us to work, the more I was pushing him further away?

I wanted to believe we were meeting in the middle. But I was always the one walking further.

Still, I held on.

I sent photos. I checked in. I reminded him of the Simba mug. I told him I missed him. I tried to recreate the magic from afar with every drop of hope I had left. But it felt like trying to light a fire with damp matches.

At first, I told myself it was just the distance.

Long workdays. Different cities. Busy schedules.

I told myself that's why his messages slowed down. That's why the warmth in his voice began to cool. That's why the emojis disappeared, and the long conversations turned into brief replies.

But deep down, I knew.

I just didn't want to know.

Eventually, the truth came out—quietly, hesitantly, like something he had been holding in for too long.

He told me he had decided to stay in Orlando.

That he wanted to build his life there. That things were starting to get easier for him—the quality of life, the slower pace, the new friendships he had made. It was all beginning to feel like home in a way New York never had. And he wanted to try. To see where it could take him. Even if it meant leaving me behind.

And the reason he had been so distant with me… Was because he didn't know how to tell me. Because he knew it would break my heart.

And it did.

I remember staring at the message, reading those words again and again, as if maybe I had misunderstood them. My eyes blurred, the screen swimming in front of me, my chest tightening until it felt like my ribs were caving in. He had already made the decision. He had already chosen a future that didn't include me—and I was the last one to find out.

It felt like someone had quietly cut the cord I'd been holding onto for so long, letting me fall without warning. My stomach dropped, my body went cold, and yet my face burned hot with a mixture of grief, humiliation, and the hollow ache of being left behind. This wasn't just losing him—it was realizing he'd been slipping away while I was still holding space for him, still believing in us, still imagining a someday that no longer existed.

There was no fight, no conversation, no moment to plead my case. Just the truth, dropped in my lap like something he'd been carrying too long and needed to set down. And now it was mine to carry. Mine to sit with. Mine to somehow survive.

It wasn't just this moment that broke me—it was the echo of every other time he had let me go without really saying the words. Every unanswered message. Every sudden silence. Every time I'd felt the shift but convinced myself it was temporary. I realized I had been here before, standing in the same emotional doorway, watching him walk away while I stayed rooted, telling myself he would come back.

This was the pattern: him slipping away quietly, me pretending not to notice until I couldn't ignore it anymore. And still, each time, I had chosen to believe in the version of him who once reached for me, who once made me feel like I was worth choosing. But now... now I couldn't hide from the truth. He had chosen. And it wasn't me.

The weight of that truth settled in my chest, heavy and unmoving, like it had always been there—like maybe I'd been carrying it all along without realizing it. I wasn't just losing him in this moment. I was losing the illusion I had built, the fragile hope I had been living inside for far too long. And without it, I didn't know what was left of me.

He didn't say it to be cruel. He said it because he didn't want to hurt me. But it hurt anyway.

Because how do you prepare for the moment someone tells you they're choosing a life that doesn't include you?

He responded, but something was missing. The softness. The care. The presence.

Every message he sent felt like it had less of him inside. And I felt it.

That quiet, familiar ache. The ache of being too much for someone who once made you feel like just enough.

I started to doubt myself. Maybe I was overthinking. Maybe I was asking for too much. Maybe I just needed to be more patient, more chill, more understanding.

I tried to convince myself that love doesn't always look the way we want it to. That some people are just bad at communicating. That he still cared—just... differently.

But the truth was harder to hold.

The truth was that I was fighting for something he had already started letting go of. And he wasn't saying it. He didn't have to.

Because you don't need words to feel someone slipping away.

You feel it in the delayed replies. In the way they stop asking how you are. In the silence that stretches longer than your excuses can cover. In the gut feeling you try to ignore—until it starts keeping you up at night.

And still, I stayed. Because staying was easier than accepting I had already been left. Because I thought if I just held on a little tighter, maybe he'd come back.

But slowly, I began to see the truth:

Sometimes, the worst kind of goodbye is the one that never gets said. It's the one you feel. The one you carry. The one you survive.

I didn't know it then, but the distance between us had already become more than miles. What came next wasn't closure—it was another almost, another fragile spark I tried to keep alive in the dark.

✦ ✦ ✦

*"Not every ending comes with words. Some just leave you
with silence, and a heart that knows it's already over."*

Chapter 11

Hope's Last Spark

"Sometimes the smallest sign can reignite the loudest hope. And when it comes from the person you love most, even silence begins to sound like a promise."

I still wasn't ready to let him go. Somewhere deep inside, I believed he wasn't ready either. Or maybe I just needed to believe that—because letting go meant admitting it was over, and I couldn't carry that truth yet.

I clung to the idea that this wasn't finished. That something still lived between us, even in the silence. Maybe it was love. Maybe it was just my longing echoing back at me. Either way, I held onto it like a lifeline, as if my heart would stop beating the moment I admitted the silence had won.

But as the weeks passed with no communication, the silence began to grow teeth. It wasn't soft anymore. It was sharp. Each day felt heavier, lonelier, as if I was walking through a world that no longer knew how to respond to my presence.

I told myself I wouldn't reach out. I rehearsed the rules over and over: *If he wants to talk, he will. If he cares, he'll show it. If he misses me, I'll know.* But every night those rules bent under the weight of my missing him. The ache pressed into my chest until it felt like breathing itself was a betrayal.

I didn't know what to say, how to start, what words could carry both my pain and my hope without spilling into desperation. But I knew I had to do something—anything—before the silence swallowed me whole.

So I did the only thing I knew how. I opened his Instagram and liked a few of his photos.

It wasn't brave. It wasn't loud. It wasn't even enough to be called reaching out.

But it was something. It was me, standing outside his door, too afraid to knock, but leaving a trace of myself on the welcome mat— hoping he'd notice. Hoping he'd remember. Hoping he'd still care.

And a few moments later, it happened.

A message from him: "I miss you so much."

I stared at it for what felt like forever. My heart burst open. Just five words—but they pulled me back in completely. I took it as a sign, a green light from the universe. This isn't over. There's still something worth holding on to. Something to fight for.

And I was ready to fight.

I didn't care how long it took. A week. A month. A year. Five years. I would wait—because there was no one else I wanted to wait for. He was the only person who felt like home. The only person I had ever loved more than I loved myself.

I knew he was building a life in Orlando. I couldn't expect too much. But if there was even the smallest chance we could find our way back to each other, I was going to take it. I would walk that path barefoot if I had to.

We started texting again. Slowly at first, then more often. The familiar rhythm returned. The hope began to grow again. I started to feel like maybe the tunnel wasn't closing—maybe the light was getting brighter.

In the back of my mind, I knew this was fragile. I knew he had made his decision to stay in Orlando. I knew the only real way to make it work would be if I moved there. But I didn't say that out loud. I kept that truth buried, afraid that even suggesting it might scare him, might make him pull away again.

He was already under so much pressure, trying to settle into a new city, a new life. The last thing I wanted was to become another source of weight. I didn't want to be too much. I didn't want to overwhelm him. I just wanted to be close—quietly, gently, without asking for anything more than connection.

And then, like something out of a story I was writing in my head, the universe opened a small door.

I was interviewing for new jobs at the time, and one company asked me to come to Miami for two days for a trial. On paper, it was a great opportunity—new role, better pay, a fresh start. But beneath all the professional excitement, my heart was already calculating the distance. Miami wasn't Orlando, but it was close. Close enough to feel like maybe fate was tilting the map in my favor, handing me one last thread to hold onto.

It felt like the universe whispering, *"Here's your chance. Don't waste it."* One more way to make this work without putting pressure on him, without asking him to change his life for me. I could bend. I could adapt. I could make this work if it meant keeping him in my orbit.

Maybe, just maybe, this could be our second chance—our third, really—but who's counting when love is on the line?

They say the third time's the charm. And honestly, at that point, I would've believed anything. If you told me water was dry, I would have nodded and said, *"So dry I need to drink something, just to get closer to him."* That's how deep I was in—how much I wanted to believe that love could still win if I just stayed open enough, patient enough, hopeful enough.

Hope had made a home in me again, curling up in the corners of my chest, feeding on every small possibility. And I didn't care how irrational it seemed. When you love someone that much, even the smallest flicker can look like a sunrise—and I was ready to chase it, no matter how far it led me.

✦ ✦ ✦

"Hope is fragile, but it's also relentless—once it sparks, it will burn until you either feed it with love or face the truth that it was never enough."

Chapter 12

Miami – The Almost

"Sometimes love doesn't return to stay—it returns to remind you that it was real, even if only for a night."

Miami felt like a possibility. A new job. A new city. A new version of me—one that still carried hope like a candle I refused to let go of, even as the wind picked up.

The invitation came suddenly, but I saw it as a sign. The opportunity was great—better pay, good people, a fresh environment. But let's be honest: the biggest reason I said yes was because it was close to him.

Just a few hours away from Orlando. Close enough to dream. Close enough to try again without saying the words out loud.

I didn't want to pressure him. I didn't want to ask for anything. I just wanted to exist near him, to breathe in the same air, to be close without making it feel like a demand. Quiet hope had become my love language.

As soon as I got official confirmation of the trip, I texted F. *"I'm coming to Miami for a job interview."*

I kept it casual, as if it were just another update—light, easy, and safe. *"Maybe I could stop by Orlando on the way back—just to say hello."*

Then I waited.

The typing bubble appeared, then vanished. Appeared again. Vanished. Each time it disappeared, my chest tightened a little more.

I told myself not to read into it, but my mind was already racing ahead, imagining every possible response—from polite distance to warm surprise.

And then it came. *"I'll come to Miami to see you."*

I froze, staring at the screen, letting the words sink in. It was simple, just one line—but it shifted everything. Suddenly, the trip wasn't just about the job. It wasn't just about possibility. It was about him. About us. About the chance to be in the same room again, to feel whatever was still there between us.

Those seven words lit something in me I hadn't felt in months. It was like a match striking in the dark—small, fleeting, but enough to make my chest ache with warmth. I could already picture it: him stepping out of a car, that familiar half-smile on his face, the way the air would shift when we were near each other again.

But hope is dangerous. It doesn't just live in you—it takes over. It starts rearranging your thoughts, tinting the future in softer colors, making you believe in things you promised yourself you'd stop believing in. I told myself to stay calm, to take it for what it was, nothing more. But deep down, I knew I was already gone.

Because when you've been starving for someone's presence, even a promise feels like a feast. And in that moment, I wasn't thinking about how it might end, or what it might cost me. I was thinking about how it might feel—to be close enough to touch him again.

He was away that week in Boston for work and was scheduled to fly back the same day we planned to meet. That alone would have been enough to make most people cancel or reschedule, but then his message came: *"I'll go home, shower, pack, and drive to you."*

I read it twice, my chest tightening. He was going to be exhausted—hours of travel behind him, a full week of work still clinging to his bones. But he was willing to drive over four hours just to see me. And in my heart, that meant more than I could explain.

It meant I still mattered. It meant maybe not everything was lost. It meant maybe he still felt something—maybe not as much as I did, but something. And when you're holding onto the edge of love, even something can feel like everything.

The day we were set to meet, I couldn't focus on anything else. My trial for the job was still in full swing, but it all felt like background noise. I went through the motions—smiling, answering questions, nodding at instructions—but none of it stuck. My mind kept drifting forward, past the interviews and the handshakes, to the moment I'd see him again.

I checked the time obsessively, each glance at the clock pulling me further out of the room I was in and into the one I wished I was. I imagined him on the road, music spilling through the speakers, his hand tapping the wheel in rhythm. I pictured the miles between us shrinking, the distance folding in on itself, until he was there—until I could look at him without a screen between us, without silence pressing in on the space where words should be.

Nothing else mattered in those hours. Not the job, not the outcome, not even the fact that I was being tested, judged, weighed by strangers who would decide my future. My heart wasn't in it. My heart was already racing down the highway toward him.

And maybe that's why, when it was all over, I didn't get the offer. Maybe they saw it in my eyes—that my mind was somewhere else, someone else. Maybe they sensed the split in me, the part that was trying to hold it together and the part that had already let go.

When the rejection came, it barely even stung. The truth was, I'd already placed my hope in something else entirely. Not in the job, not in the paycheck, but in him—in us.

And that was the gamble: I had staked my future on a meeting that hadn't even happened yet.

I changed hotels for the night—booked a nicer one. I wanted us to be comfortable. I wanted to make it special. Perfect, if I could. As the clock ticked toward his arrival, I couldn't sit still. I went out to get food, unsure of what he'd want. Sushi? Fruit? Snacks? I bought too much—of course I did. I just wanted him to have everything he might need. I wanted to take care of him. I wanted him to feel, even in silence, how much he meant to me.

By the time evening came, my chest was a tight knot of nerves and longing. I got ready like it was the first time all over again—choosing my clothes with care, making sure every detail was just right. I told myself it was for me, for confidence, but really, it was for him. To remind him of what we'd been. To remind myself that I could still feel this way.

Just after 9 p.m., my phone lit up with his message: *"I'm here."*

My pulse spiked instantly. I smoothed my shirt, took a breath I didn't realize I'd been holding, and started toward the entrance—each step pulling me deeper into the moment I'd been replaying in my mind since the day he said he'd come.

When I saw him, my breath caught. His AC had broken on the drive, and he'd been riding for hours with the windows down. I could see the exhaustion in his eyes—but the moment he smiled, it all disappeared. Tired, but still him. Eyes locking with mine, that half-smile curling like he'd been waiting for this too.

In that instant, the noise of Miami faded. The job, the miles, the months of silence—none of it mattered. All that mattered was that he was here, in front of me, and I could finally reach out and feel the truth in the space between us.

He stepped toward me, and for a second, I forgot how to breathe. We didn't rush it—there was a moment of stillness, like we were both trying to read the other's face, to see what had changed and what had stayed the same. Then his arms were around me, and I was home. I pressed my cheek against his shoulder, breathing him in, the faint trace of his cologne threading through the warm scent of him. He held me firmly, like he didn't want to let go just yet, and I let myself melt into that embrace, letting months of distance collapse in an instant. My hands gripped the back of his shirt, half afraid that if I loosened my hold, he might vanish.

When we finally pulled back, our eyes met and lingered. He gave me a tired smile—the kind that said more than words could—and brushed his thumb lightly over my arm as if to prove I was really there.

"Hey," he said softly. *"Hey,"* I echoed, my voice barely above a whisper.

It was simple, almost nothing. But in that small exchange, there was everything—months of absence, and a thousand things neither of us knew how to say out loud.

We went to the room. He was hungry and, of course, chose the sushi. I smiled—it was a good choice. I didn't eat much. I was too full of nerves, too full of feeling. I just sat beside him in quiet happiness, watching him, memorizing the way his mouth curved when he chewed, the sound of his voice, the way his presence filled the room without trying.

After he ate and freshened up, we took the champagne outside.

The hotel had a pool area wrapped in gardens and soft, golden lights that seemed to float in the air. It was late—the kind of late where the world feels slowed down, like even time is taking a breath. The only sounds were the faint hum of crickets in the distance and the gentle ripple of water shifting under the glow. We were the only ones there—just us and the shimmer of the pool, the air still warm enough to kiss your skin without a shiver. The city felt far away, as if it had dissolved beyond the horizon, leaving us in our own hidden corner of the universe.

It felt safe there. Like the world had decided to pause, to hold space just for us.

The magic returned, quietly but completely—slipping back in the way sunlight spills into a dark room at dawn, touching everything softly as if afraid it might break.

I looked at him and felt something swell in my chest—hope, maybe. Or the echo of it. That dangerous, beautiful thought that maybe this was a turning point, that maybe we had found our way back to something we'd lost. I didn't say it out loud. I didn't dare. Moments like this are too delicate to name—they crumble if you hold them too tightly.

And for a moment—it was perfect again. The way it used to be. The way I had always wanted it to stay.

I was scared. I knew it was temporary. I knew this might be our last flicker. But I didn't want to waste it wondering. I didn't want to ruin the present by clinging to the future. So I made a choice: to be here, to be still, to let this night wrap around me and hold me while it lasted.

After the champagne, we returned to the room. It was tucked away on the ground level, quiet and secluded, with a small private patio that felt like it belonged only to us. A hot tub waited just outside, steam curling into the night air, carrying the promise of warmth and something more.

We looked at each other, and the decision didn't need words. It was there in the way his eyes lingered on mine, in the subtle tilt of his head, in the quiet exhale that seemed to dissolve whatever space was left between us. We stepped outside together, the warm night brushing against our skin, sharpening the electricity already moving between us.

Before we even got in, our hands found each other. Not tentative, not searching, but certain—like magnets snapping back into place after too long apart. His fingers slid against mine, steady and warm, and in that single touch I felt all the unspoken things we hadn't been able to say out loud. The silences. The waiting. The ache of distance. All of it lived in the way his hand closed around mine.

The night wrapped around us like a secret. The bubbling water whispered in the background, but neither of us moved toward it right away. We just stood there for a moment—barely breathing, holding on—because sometimes it isn't the kiss or the embrace that carries the weight, but the simple act of choosing to touch and not let go.

There was a hunger between us that had never really gone away— just slept beneath the surface. The kind of hunger that lives in your skin, your memory, your longing. He touched me like he had missed me, like he had dreamed of this too. Our lips met, urgent and soft, and I felt myself unravel.

Clothes fell away, one by one, like pieces of fear shedding from our bodies. I didn't care who could see. I didn't care about anything outside that moment. All I wanted was him—his skin, his breath, his mouth, his hands.

We slipped into the hot tub, steam rising around us like a curtain pulling us into our own world. He pulled me close, and we made love with a kind of aching passion that felt like both reunion and goodbye. It wasn't just physical. It was emotional. It was sacred. It was everything we hadn't said, everything we still wanted, everything we were too afraid to ask for, spoken through touch.

It felt like the first time again—in my apartment, when the world was still new and untouched by heartbreak. It brought back memories, emotions, a version of myself I hadn't seen in a long time.

In his arms, I came back to life.

And in the back of my heart, I knew… This night would live inside me forever. Even if he didn't.

The next morning, sunlight filtered through the thin hotel curtains—soft, indifferent. It crept across the floor, across the sheets, and onto our skin, touching us without asking how the night had gone. Without caring what it meant. The world outside was already moving on, already rushing into a new day, but in that room, time felt slower—like it was giving us a fragile grace period before reality found its way back in.

He was still next to me, lying quietly, eyes closed. His breath was steady, almost delicate, the rise and fall of his chest like a rhythm my heart wanted to match. I watched him, letting my eyes trace the familiar lines of him—the curve of his back, the shape of his shoulders, the softness in his face that only appeared when sleep erased the weight he carried when awake.

I wanted to memorize it. To burn it into me so deeply that even if everything else slipped away, this moment would remain intact, untouchable. I wanted to stay in that stillness. To freeze it. To convince time to be kind to me for once.

But even as I lay there, I felt the truth pressing in from the edges—that this was temporary. That mornings like this were not promises, but pauses. I held my breath, afraid that opening my mouth, even to whisper something gentle, might break the spell. So instead, I just watched him breathe, silently bargaining with the universe to let me keep him a little longer.

Because sometimes love isn't loud or certain. Sometimes it's fragile, fleeting—something you hold with trembling hands, knowing it could slip away the second you try to grasp it too tightly.

I don't know how long I stayed there, just watching him—measuring the world by the rise and fall of his chest. But then, slowly, he stirred. His fingers shifted against the sheets, his body stretching slightly, and his eyelids fluttered open.

For a second, he looked almost disoriented, caught between dreams and waking. Then his eyes found mine. And just like that, the silence changed.

He gave a small, sleepy smile—so faint it almost wasn't there, but enough to undo me. Enough to make my chest ache with both gratitude and fear. Gratitude, because I still had him beside me in that moment. Fear, because I didn't know how many more mornings like this there would be.

"Morning," he whispered, his voice rough, soft, unguarded.

"Morning," I whispered back, afraid that speaking too loud might shatter the stillness we had created.

Neither of us moved right away. The sunlight had grown brighter, creeping higher across the bed, reminding us that the day was waiting. But for those few minutes, we resisted it. We lay there, facing each other, speaking only with small touches—the brush of his hand against mine, the way his knee bent closer, the warmth that lingered between us.

It wasn't a declaration. It wasn't a promise. But it was something real. And sometimes, the quietest moments carry the loudest truths.

We still had the day ahead of us—at least until 3 p.m. when we had to check out—so we decided to spend it by the pool. It was a beautiful, sunny Miami day. Our last day. And even though the magic of the night before still lingered in the air, part of me already felt the clock ticking.

Before we had fallen asleep the night before, he had turned to me and asked, *"Do you want to come to Orlando with me tomorrow?"*

I didn't even think twice. Of course, I said yes. Is that even a question?

His invitation felt like a thread being tied between us again—a new beginning, or at least the possibility of one. I didn't want to overthink it. I didn't want to wonder what it meant. I just wanted to feel it. So I let myself.

We got up, packed a little, and headed to the pool. The sun was already blazing, and the space quickly filled with hotel guests trying to soak up the day. There was no privacy, no quiet like the night before—but I didn't care. No one else existed to me but him. As long as I was next to him, nothing else mattered.

We swam, sunbathed, and dipped into the pool every time the heat became too much. And every time we were in the water, our hands found each other again. It wasn't overt. It wasn't showy. But it was there—real, unspoken, electric.

Later, when we got hungry, we ordered food by the pool. I'll never forget the moment he fed me pieces of coconut—soft and sweet and simple. It was such a small gesture, but it felt like everything.

Then a stranger lounging near us leaned over and asked, *"Are you two together? Like, boyfriends?"*

I froze. We weren't together. Not officially. Not really. I didn't know what to say. I started fumbling for something neutral, diplomatic—but before I could answer, he turned to them and said casually: *"Yes. He's my boyfriend."*

My heart jumped.

For a moment, it beat so fast I thought I might lose my breath. But then it slowed, because I realized—he probably only said it to make the conversation end. To avoid more questions. To keep things simple.

Or maybe he meant it. Maybe just for a second, he really felt it. Maybe he wanted it too. I don't know. And maybe I'll never know.

✦ ✦ ✦

"Some nights don't promise a forever—but they give you something just as precious: a memory soft enough to hold, and real enough to feel like love."

Chapter 13

Borrowed Words

*"Sometimes a single word can feel like a lifetime.
Sometimes a lifetime disappears into silence."*

All I wanted was to remember that moment. Those words. *"Yes. He's my boyfriend."*

Even if they weren't entirely true. Even if they were just for show, spoken casually in front of others to avoid questions, to keep things simple, to fill in the blanks that labels are supposed to solve.

Because for me, it didn't matter why he said it. What mattered was that, for the briefest stretch of time, the world saw us as I had always seen us. As I had always wanted us to be. My heart had been aching for that recognition, for those words to leave his lips—even if they weren't meant in the way I dreamed.

And when they did, I clung to them like a drowning man clutching driftwood.

Because for that moment, I got to hear the one thing I had wanted more than anything. To belong to him. To not just feel it in stolen glances and quiet touches, but to hear it spoken out loud. A truth, even if it was only make-believe.

I held onto that moment like it was something sacred, pressing it into my memory with desperate hands, terrified it might slip through the cracks if I didn't hold tight enough. I replayed it in my head again and again, because it felt like proof—proof that somewhere, in some corner of him, he must have known what I was to him.

Even if it was fleeting. Even if it would never come again. Even if I had to live with the bitter sweetness of knowing that the words I longed for most were also the ones that would haunt me.

Because sometimes love is nothing more than a handful of seconds you can never get back—moments that mean everything to you and almost nothing to the person who gave them.

At first, I floated in it. The sound of his voice saying those words echoed in me like a hymn, like something holy I'd been waiting years to hear. My chest swelled, and for a moment I let myself believe it—believe that I was his, that he had chosen me, that what I felt wasn't one-sided after all.

But then the silence that followed began to unravel it. The way he didn't look at me after. The way his hand didn't reach for mine. The way the word *boyfriend* dissolved into the air like smoke, leaving no trace behind.

I wanted to ask him if he meant it. If, even for a second, he had believed it too. But I didn't. Because deep down, I already knew the answer. It wasn't a confession. It wasn't a promise. It was convenience. A shield. Something easy to say in a moment where questions might have burned too close to the truth.

And yet—I couldn't let go of it. I carried it with me like contraband, hidden away in the deepest pocket of my heart, replaying it whenever the silence between us grew too loud. I twisted it into comfort, even though it cut me every time.

Because the cruelest part of love is that sometimes the smallest scraps feel like a feast when you've been starving.

And that afternoon, those words fed me.

And in my hunger, I made a meal out of them.

Even as they hollowed me out.

For a while, I lived off those words like they were mine to keep. I tucked them into the softest corners of my memory, pulling them out when the ache became unbearable—when his distance settled over me like rejection, when the quiet between us made me doubt if any of it had been real. I let them soothe me, even though they weren't built to last, even though they were never meant to carry the weight I placed on them.

Because sometimes, love doesn't survive in the big declarations. Sometimes, it survives in fragments—borrowed words, fleeting gestures, moments that were never promised but felt like everything anyway.

But memories have sharp edges, and the more I held onto them, the more they cut. The more I replayed it, the clearer it became—he hadn't said it because he meant it. He said it because it was easy. Because it saved him from questions he didn't want to answer. Because in that moment, it cost him nothing to give me everything I had been dying to hear.

And that realization stung in a way I can't explain. It was like holding a gift that sparkled in the dark, only to find out it was made of glass—beautiful, fragile, and destined to shatter if I tried to claim it as mine.

So I learned to let it go. Slowly. Painfully.

I stopped twisting it into proof of something deeper. I stopped using it as a shield against the truth I didn't want to face. I began to see it for what it was: a moment, not a promise. A word, not a vow.

And in that acceptance, there was grief. But there was also clarity.

Because as much as I wanted to keep building a life out of scraps, I knew I deserved more than borrowed words spoken for convenience.

I deserved a love that didn't need pretending, a love that didn't sting in the morning light, a love that could stand without disguises or half-truths. Something that wasn't fragile or conditional, but steady, certain, and real.

Still—somewhere deep inside, a part of me never forgot the way it felt to hear it, even just once.

The sweetness and the ache lived side by side inside me, refusing to let go of each other. It was a strange kind of duality: joy at having touched the dream, pain at knowing it wasn't mine to keep. That single word—*boyfriend*—became both a balm and a blade, healing me and hurting me at the same time.

It reminded me of the depth of my love, of how far I was willing to go to hold onto even a sliver of him. But it also reminded me of the cost—what it meant to love someone so much that you'd cling to illusions, feeding yourself on shadows and echoes.

And that was the cruelest truth of all: that sometimes the things we treasure most are the very things that undo us.

For so long, I let that moment define me. I let it convince me that I was almost enough—that if I just held on tighter, if I stayed patient, if I proved my love quietly and endlessly, maybe the scraps would turn into something whole.

But love built on almosts will always collapse. And eventually, I had to face that truth.

I began to see how much of myself I had poured into him, how much of my worth I had measured in the tilt of his attention, in the pauses between his replies, in the way he sometimes reached for me and sometimes didn't. I had mistaken the silence for mystery, when in reality it was absence. I had mistaken convenience for care, when in truth it was only comfort—for him, not me.

And I realized: I couldn't keep living this way. I couldn't keep starving myself, convincing my heart that crumbs were a feast.

Because beneath the ache of wanting him was an even deeper ache—the one that came from abandoning myself.

So I started the slow, messy work of choosing differently. Of choosing me.

It wasn't clean. It wasn't easy. Some days I still replayed the memory like it was gospel. Some nights I still clung to it like it had the power to save me. But even through the grief, I understood something I hadn't before: I deserved to stop living on scraps.

I deserved a love that didn't vanish with the morning light. I deserved a love that stayed.

I clung to those words like they could carry me forward, even when I knew they weren't enough. Sometimes, almost feels like home—until you remember you can't live inside a maybe.

✦ ✦ ✦

"Real love doesn't ask you to starve. It feeds you, freely, and it stays."

Chapter 14

Almost Home

*"Sometimes endings don't come with slammed
doors or sharp words. Sometimes they arrive
quietly, in the spaces where love used to live."*

The sun was beginning to set over Miami, casting everything in that golden, gentle glow—the kind that makes you wish you could pause time. That light became our signal. It was time to pack up and start the drive to Orlando.

We showered, zipped up our bags, and headed to the car. The last night and day had been perfect, and I genuinely believed nothing could ruin that feeling. My happiness was growing louder with every mile marker we passed. At that moment, I felt something I hadn't in a long time—something rare, almost childlike: pure, unfiltered joy.

I was with the love of my life, on the way to see his new home. I sat in his car, by his side, with the kind of hopeful heart that believes—against all reason—that maybe this time, things were finally falling into place.

The road stretched endlessly before us, lined with trees that bent toward the light, as if even they were reaching for something just out of grasp. The air carried the heaviness of the day—hours under the sun had left us tired, our bodies worn—but the tiredness didn't matter. We filled the silence with laughter, with music that wove between us like an old friend, with glances that carried the ease of familiarity. And in those moments, it felt like we had stepped back into something lost but never forgotten. Like maybe, just maybe, we'd circled back to where we belonged.

Then came the gesture I'll never forget: his hand rested gently on my leg as we drove. He didn't speak. He didn't have to. That touch said everything I had been waiting months to hear. It told me I was seen. It told me I still mattered. It wrapped around my heart like a shield against all the nights I had cried alone, against every unanswered message, every silence that had cut sharper than words. For those few seconds, I wasn't just hoping anymore—I was living the hope made real.

I let myself sink into it. I let myself believe. I leaned into the fragile warmth as if it could carry me home. But beneath the sweetness was a tremor I couldn't ignore. I knew the way our story worked: perfect moments never lasted. They bloomed quickly, beautifully, like wild-flowers after rain, only to wither in the sun of reality. Still, I clung to it. I clung as if holding tighter could change the ending I already sensed.

Because somewhere deep inside, even as his hand steadied me, I could feel it—the undertow of distance waiting to return, the silence I knew would eventually stretch between us again. It was always there, hiding in the shadows of our brightest hours. And though I wanted to believe we were finally finding our way back, part of me already knew: this was not a beginning. It was another beautiful interlude in a story that never learned how to stay whole.

Perfect moments don't last here. Not in our story. They never did.

When we arrived in Orlando, something shifted.

All throughout the drive, I had been clinging to this picture in my head: the two of us finally resting, finally breathing, finally allowing ourselves to just *be*. I thought we'd spend the night together, shut out the noise of the world, let the exhaustion of the trip melt into close-ness. I imagined us unwinding with laughter, collapsing into bed, and waking up slowly the next morning, still wrapped in each other the way I had always wanted us to be. For me, Orlando was supposed to be a beginning, a chance to feel chosen.

But he had other plans. He didn't ask what I wanted, didn't pause to consider the softness I had been quietly aching for. With a tone that left no room for hesitation, he told me we were going out to meet his friends. Just like that, the night I had built in my mind unraveled before it even began.

I didn't argue. I smiled, told him I'd love to, because that's what I did—I hid my disappointment behind eagerness. And maybe it wasn't all pretend. A part of me truly did want to meet them. Maybe it meant something that he wanted to include me, that he wasn't hiding me away this time. Maybe it was a sign that I mattered enough to step into his world.

But underneath the surface of that hope was the familiar spiral of questions I never dared to voice. Would he call me his boyfriend? Would he claim me as more than just a friend? Would he finally let people see us the way I had always seen us? My heart raced with possibilities, fragile and intoxicating, even as my chest tightened with the fear that the answer would be no.

I told myself to wait, to be patient, to let the night unfold. But as we left for his friends, the quiet dream of intimacy I had been holding onto slipped further and further away. And I couldn't shake the feeling that this was the real story of us: me, always hoping for more; him, always steering us somewhere else.

The original plan was to drive to Tampa, but at the last minute, he changed his mind, and we ended up at a bar in Orlando instead. I didn't question it—I rarely did. His choices always carried the night, and I followed, telling myself it was easier that way.

To my surprise, the evening turned out to be fun. His friends were warm and easy to talk to, and for a while, it felt like I was being welcomed into something bigger than just him and me. Their laughter made space for me, their questions felt genuine, and I caught myself thinking—*maybe this is it. Maybe this is how I finally become part of his world.* For a fleeting stretch of time, I let myself believe I wasn't on the outside looking in anymore. I was being let in. I was part of his life.

But beneath that thin layer of joy was the truth: I was exhausted. My body was heavy, my head buzzing with the toll of the day. More than anything, I just wanted to go home with him—his home, our night, our bed. I wanted the intimacy of silence, the safety of curling into him, the simple proof that closeness still belonged to us.

Instead, when the night wound down, we ended up at his friend's place. He explained casually, as if it was no big deal, and I followed again. His friend, kind and generous, offered us his bedroom while he took the couch. It was thoughtful, but strange. The bed felt too unfamiliar, too borrowed, like we were guests in a life that wasn't ours.

I barely had time to adjust before we slipped under the covers. The day had drained us both, and whatever spark I had been carrying quietly all night dissolved into fatigue. We cuddled—soft, brief, unspoken—and then drifted into sleep. No long talks, no kisses that lingered, no closeness that matched the picture I had been holding onto all day. Just the quiet weight of him beside me, and the sharp awareness that even when he was next to me, I still felt a little far away.

The next morning, I woke early—like I always do. Sleep rarely stays with me long. I lay there, next to F, watching him sleep. The rise and fall of his chest. The way the light hit his face. I studied him like I was memorizing the last page of a book I didn't want to close.

When he woke up, he smiled at me. Kissed me. It was sweet. Soft. Familiar.

And then, coffee—strong and black, exactly what I needed. He brought it to me with that easy charm that always made my heart flutter, even when I didn't want it to.

We cuddled, started watching *Cruella,* and for a moment, it felt like we were in our own little world again. But not even an hour into the movie, he left. Quietly. Casually. He went to hang out with his friend in the living room, and just like that—I was alone in a stranger's bed with a cooling coffee and a movie I was now watching for no reason.

A wave of sadness hit me.

But then I caught myself. *Don't be sad,* I told myself. *Be grateful. You're here. With him.* That should be enough.

The rain outside kept us in most of the day. Eventually, when it cleared, the three of us went out to eat. I was surprised he didn't want it to be just the two of us. It was supposed to be our time. But again—I said nothing. I had already buried too many questions. I was too afraid of the answers.

So I smiled. Laughed at the right times. Played the part of someone who wasn't slowly realizing: I might be more in love than he ever was.

And even if he cared, even if he tried—I was starting to see that maybe, just maybe, I was trying harder.

Later that evening, we finally left his friend's place and drove back to his apartment. I hoped, maybe now, we'd have a moment just for us. Something quiet. Something simple. Something that reminded us of what we were trying to hold onto.

But when we got back, the distance was already there—unspoken, but heavy. We didn't talk about anything real. We didn't talk about us. He was tired. I was quiet. And the space between us, the emotional one, felt wider than it had before Miami.

Once we got to his place, we barely had time to rest. We changed quickly, and before I could catch my breath, we were heading out again—more plans, more friends. I didn't ask questions. I didn't want to be difficult. I just followed his lead, forced a smile, and told myself this was fine.

But it wasn't.

Underneath the smile was sadness that I couldn't contain anymore. I didn't understand what was happening. How did we go from that soft, romantic glow in Miami to this—cold, distant, distracted? How did it all shift so fast?

I didn't ask. I knew I wouldn't get the answer that night. So I shook it off and tried to enjoy what I knew was likely our last night together. Deep down, I was hoping he'd ask me to stay longer. I would've. In a heartbeat. But he didn't.

We picked up his friend and went out to a couple of nearby bars. The night blurred quickly. We took ecstasy together, hoping it would make the night lighter, freer. It always made me emotional, and tonight I didn't need any help with that—but I took it anyway. I wanted to feel closer to him. I wanted anything that might pull us back together.

At first, it worked. The music was good. The energy was soft and strange in that dreamy way only ecstasy can bring. But slowly, more friends arrived, and I found myself on the outside. Watching him laugh with them, stand beside them, give them the presence he wasn't giving me.

I stood there, fading.

The drug made every moment louder. More raw. More exposed. I tried not to cry, but I was crumbling inside. I kept wondering: *Why is he doing this? Why am I here if I'm invisible to him?*

When the night ended, I thought we'd finally go home—*his* home. The place I'd been imagining since the drive, the place I thought we were heading toward together. But no. Once again, we went back to his friend's house. Another borrowed bed. Another night that wasn't ours. Another night that didn't feel like love, only like I was being tucked into the margins of his life.

And then it got worse. He didn't even ride back with me. Instead, he drove his friend, who was drunk, leaving me to ride with his other friend—the one we were staying with. Someone I barely knew. A stranger in every way that mattered. I told myself it was fine, that it was practical, that maybe it even said something good about him—that he was being responsible. But the truth was, it hurt. It hurt that I wasn't the one he chose to sit beside. That, once again, I was left waiting.

We arrived back first, and the house was quiet. Too quiet. I sat there in the unfamiliar living room, the strangeness of it pressing down on me. Minutes ticked by. I checked my phone. Nothing. My mind began to spin—*Where were they? Why hadn't he texted?* The longer the silence stretched, the heavier it felt, until it was crushing me.

Finally, a message came through. Just four words: *We stopped to eat.*

No explanation. No invitation. No apology. Just casual indifference, typed out like it was nothing. And maybe to him it was nothing—but to me, it was everything. The man I loved had gone to eat without me, leaving me waiting, small and invisible, in a stranger's home.

The sadness that hit me wasn't loud. It didn't demand attention. It didn't even bring tears. It was quieter than that, heavier. It was the kind of sadness that hollowed you out from the inside, that left you sitting still, staring at nothing, because moving felt pointless. I felt abandoned. Forgotten. Like the place I had been hoping to fill in his life didn't even exist.

And in that silence, I realized something I had been avoiding for too long: love shouldn't feel this lonely.

They arrived later. He didn't say sorry. He hugged me like nothing happened, like I hadn't spent the past hour spiraling in that silence. He asked me to come to bed with him. I didn't want to. I was too hurt. Too confused. But I had nowhere else to go.

So I followed him, again. Into that room. Into that bed. But there was no closeness that night. No touch. No warmth. Just silence. Just distance. Just two people lying side by side, as far apart as they'd ever been.

I couldn't sleep.

Neither could he, it seemed. I saw him on his phone, texting in the dark. Over and over. With someone I didn't know. I didn't ask. I didn't dare.

I told myself it must be important. I told myself I needed to trust him. I tried to believe there was a reason. But the truth is, it hurt. It cut. To lie next to someone you love so deeply, and feel completely unseen.

He didn't reach for me that night. Didn't hold me. Didn't kiss my shoulder like he used to. I turned away and closed my eyes, pretending to sleep.

But I didn't.

I lay there awake, in a stranger's bed, beside the man I loved, feeling like the biggest stranger of all.

The next morning came slowly. The kind of slow that aches.

I opened my eyes before the sun had fully risen. He was still asleep beside me, turned away. There was a time not long ago when waking up next to him filled me with light. That morning, it felt like watching a dream dissolve before I could hold on to it.

I got up quietly and gathered my things. I didn't want to wake him—not out of tenderness, but because I couldn't face another good-bye that felt like nothing. I wasn't sure I could survive one more silent departure, one more hug that didn't mean stay.

Eventually, he woke. Still quiet. Still distant.

We moved around each other like strangers in a borrowed room—polite, careful, distant. Not lovers. Not even friends. Just two people occupying the same silence.

He drove us back to his place. The car ride was mostly quiet, filled with questions I didn't dare ask out loud. I stared out the window as the city blurred past, wishing I could stop time, rewind it, or just understand how we'd gotten here. I wanted to ask, *did I do something wrong?* But I already knew the answer.

I didn't do anything wrong.

We still had a few hours before my flight. We sat in his room, side by side, saying almost nothing. The silence was heavy—thick enough to taste. I tried to hold my emotions in, to keep my face still, to pretend I was fine. But it was a lie. I could feel the pressure building inside me, like a bucket filled past its edge, trembling with the weight, just waiting for the smallest shift to make it spill over.

And without warning, it did.

The tears came fast, uninvited, hot against my cheeks. I didn't want them. I bit the inside of my cheek, willing them to stop, but the more I fought, the harder they came. My chest tightened, my throat ached, and all the words I'd swallowed over the last day began to rise to the surface.

He looked over, startled. *"Is everything okay?"* he asked. *"No,"* I said quietly, my voice shaking. *"It's not."*

The dam broke. *"How do you think everything's okay? After last night? After the way you left me alone at your friend's house, like I didn't matter?"*

His face shifted instantly—something between defensiveness and irritation. His posture stiffened, his eyes sharp.

"He's my friend," he said flatly. *"I love him. I had to take care of him."*

And just like that, the bullet landed.

It wasn't the fact that he loved his friend. It wasn't even the words themselves. It was what they revealed—that I wasn't someone who needed caring for. Not to him. Not anymore.

Something inside me splintered. I felt it physically—like a thin piece of glass cracking right in the center of my chest, the soundless shatter sending shards through me. I wanted to scream, to tell him I had needed him more than I'd ever admit out loud, that his absence in that moment had felt like abandonment dressed up as loyalty to someone else. But I couldn't. My mouth wouldn't form the words. My body felt hollow, my heart too heavy to lift.

Right then, I knew.

That was the end of us.

Not with a scream. Not with a slammed door. But with that sentence—sharp, careless, final. It was like watching the last ember of a fire die out, knowing no amount of oxygen could bring it back.

All I wanted in that moment was to disappear. To be invisible. To run. To go home and bury myself in the safety of solitude, where no one could leave me standing in the cold ever again. But even as I sat there, still beside him, I realized I was already alone.

Later, I would understand that it wasn't just about that night. It was about every moment before it that I had tucked away, telling myself not to make it a big deal. Every time he'd pulled away when I needed him close. Every unanswered message. Every plan that fell through without explanation. Every time I'd been left on the outskirts of his world, trying to convince myself I was still part of it.

This moment—the way he looked at me, the way he spoke—wasn't an isolated wound. It was the sum of all the little cuts that had come before, finally deep enough to hit the bone. And the worst part wasn't the anger or the sadness. It was the clarity. The sudden, undeniable knowing that I had been asking for something he no longer wanted to give. That maybe he hadn't wanted to for a long time.

It hurt in a way that felt final. Not a sharp burst of pain, but a slow, aching hollow that spread through my chest and settled there, heavy and unmovable. And in that stillness, I understood: it wasn't just that he couldn't care for me in that moment. It was that he no longer saw me as someone worth caring for at all.

I didn't say much after that. What was there to say? The conversation was already over, even if we were still sitting in the same room. I stared at the floor, at my hands, at anything that would keep me from meeting his eyes—because I knew if I did, I'd see the truth I wasn't ready to carry.

The air between us felt thin, almost fragile, like one more word might shatter it completely. But silence didn't save me. It just let the truth settle deeper, until it became part of me.

I kept breathing, kept sitting there, kept pretending I could hold myself together. But inside, something had already folded in on itself. The part of me that had been reaching for him for so long was finally still. Not because it wanted to be—because it had no choice.

That was the end of us.

Not with a fight. Not with a goodbye.

But with the quiet, unshakable certainty that he was already gone.

He drove me to the airport.

We didn't speak.

And when it was time to go—time to leave him, maybe forever—I gave him one last hug. I memorized it, just in case. I smiled through the tears I didn't want him to see. And then I walked away.

He said, *"I'm here if you need anything. I'll see you soon."*

But I didn't respond. I didn't turn around. I just walked.

Away from him. Away from us. And into the beginning of the hardest kind of healing—

The kind where no one apologizes. The kind where no one says goodbye. The kind where you leave… because staying means losing yourself.

"Sometimes surrender isn't giving up—it's the most faithful way to love, even when love has nowhere left to live but inside you."

Chapter 15

Almost isn't enough

"The saddest thing about love is that it can be
everything, and still not be enough."

The entire way back home, and long after I arrived, I kept replaying everything in my head—trying to piece it all together, trying to understand what had gone wrong. I was hurt. Heartbroken. And completely lost in confusion.

What happened?

I searched for answers, and when none came, I turned the blame inward. Maybe I was too much. Maybe I pushed too hard. Maybe my emotions overwhelmed him. Maybe I scared him off by caring too deeply, too soon.

I thought—if only I had played it cooler, stayed quiet, held back a little longer… maybe he wouldn't have pulled away. Maybe he would've seen me as steady instead of intense, soft instead of fragile.

Maybe he thought—*If he's this emotional now, what would it be like if we were truly together?*

I don't know. And I probably never will.

But now, looking back with time and distance between us, I can see things more clearly. There were cracks on both sides.

He couldn't handle how close I was getting, and I couldn't slow down. I wanted everything. All at once. I wanted to love and be loved fully, loudly, endlessly. And I see now that might have been too much for him in that moment.

But still—he could have said something. We could have talked. We could have tried to understand each other. Instead, we stayed quiet.

We let the silence grow. We drowned inside all the things we didn't say.

And in that silence, I learned something heartbreaking and true: Love is not enough.

Not without communication. Not without understanding. Not without choosing each other, intentionally, again and again. Not without the courage to say, *"This is what I need,"* or the tenderness to ask, *"How are you really feeling?"*

We had moments—beautiful, unforgettable moments. But we lived inside those moments instead of building something beyond them.

We forgot to talk about what we needed. We forgot to ask each other how we were really feeling. We let the highs carry us and ignored the quiet questions that were waiting in the spaces between.

And once trust slips, once the foundation begins to crack, it's hard—so hard—to rebuild.

If we had just communicated better... maybe it could have been different.

But we didn't. And sometimes, the saddest truth is that two people can feel everything for each other... and still fall apart.

I didn't know it then, but that trip to Orlando was the final flicker of our flame. It wasn't a dramatic ending—no screaming, no final text, no clear goodbye. Just the slow fading of something that once felt like everything.

And maybe that's what made it hurt more. Because when love doesn't break loudly, it echoes quietly... in the spaces where laughter used to live, in the silence between messages, in the way you stop reaching out because you're too afraid of the quiet that might answer.

It's in those empty spaces that I finally understood: We didn't know how to talk to each other about the hard things.

We were so good at feeling, at being in the moment, at getting swept up in the high. But we were strangers when it came to expressing doubt, fear, uncertainty, or need.

I thought if I loved him enough, if I held on tightly enough, he would know. But people aren't mind readers.

No matter how strong the connection, if we don't speak, misunderstandings will always fill the silence. Assumptions will write the story we never got brave enough to tell out loud.

We needed honesty. We needed vulnerability, not just in touch, but in words. We needed the kind of communication that creates safety—not just passion.

Instead, we stayed quiet. And in that quiet, everything slipped away.

Love can light the fire. But without communication, it burns out. Without words, without clarity, without the mutual willingness to build something real and steady—it flickers, it gasps for air, and it eventually dies.

That was the beginning of the end.

And even though part of me still wanted to believe, still clung to the hope that something might shift, the truth had already begun to settle like dust around my heart.

We were almost something. We were almost forever. We were… almost home.

But almost isn't enough. Not when your heart has nowhere left to go.

I didn't lose him all at once. It wasn't a crash. It was a slow unraveling—a quiet slipping of fingers that once held on too tightly, now brushing past each other in silence.

There was no final blow, no big fight, no shattering moment. Just a slow dimming of light, a slow turning away, until one day, I was reaching out and he just… wasn't there.

And still, I never stopped loving him.

The truth is, he hurt me. More than once. In ways that cut deep, in moments that left me crying alone in rooms where I should've felt safe. But I know now—he never meant to hurt me. Not really. Not intentionally. He was just doing the best he could, with the tools he had, in the only way he knew how.

I see that now. I didn't see it then—not because I didn't want to, but because I was too wrapped up in my own needs, my own pain, my own idea of what love should look like.

I had this version of us in my mind—perfect, romantic, unstoppable. I clung to that idea so tightly that I couldn't see the reality of who he was, of where we really were.

I see him now. I see how he tried in his own way. In small gestures, in quiet consistency, in the fact that he showed up when he could—even when he couldn't give me everything I asked for.

He didn't always have the words, but sometimes his actions whispered what his voice couldn't say.

And I wish—God, I wish—I had been able to tell him this back then:

"I understand why you pull away sometimes. I'm still here for you. You are safe with me." "I see that you're trying—even if it doesn't always show. I appreciate your efforts." "I'm not going to leave just because things get hard. We can figure it out together." "I know closeness can feel overwhelming. It's okay. I'll be here when you're ready. No pressure. Just space. Just love." "It's okay to be vulnerable with me. You don't have to have it all figured out. I won't judge you."

I wish I had said these things and many more. I wish I had communicated better. I wish I had spoken my feelings instead of holding everything in.

I wish I could've loved him out loud in the way he needed—not just in the way I knew how.

But the truth is, I was scared, too. Scared of losing him. Scared of being too much. Scared of not being enough.

So I clung, I demanded, I reached for him harder... and he pulled away further.

And during that time—lost, confused, aching—I remember one night sitting alone, headphones on, and The Kelly Family's *"I Can't Help Myself"* started playing. A song from my childhood, now echoing every corner of my pain.

It said everything I couldn't. My heart was screaming, *"Don't say goodbye,"* even if no one could hear it—especially him. The lyrics poured into me like a prayer I didn't know I was holding.

That song stayed with me for a long time, haunting and beautiful, reminding me of both the best and worst moments of us—but always, always... filled with love.

"If I would tell you How much you mean to me I think you wouldn't understand it So I'll wait, I'll wait until This day comes When you will understand it"

"Ooooooh, don't say goodbye"

That melody played like a confession my mouth never formed. And maybe he would never understand how deeply I felt. Maybe I was too much. Or maybe I just loved differently—louder, messier, fuller.

But it was real. It was mine.

I wanted to be his home. I still do.

And even though our love story didn't survive, even though we couldn't make it last—I will always love him for who he is. Fully. Honestly. Without needing him to change. Without needing him to be anything more or less than exactly himself.

He is a good person. He always has been. And more than anything, I just wanted to be part of his life. As a boyfriend. As a friend. As someone he passed on the street every few years and smiled at because he remembered how deeply we once loved.

I just didn't want to lose him—not completely.

I don't know what the future holds for us. And for once, I don't want to guess. I don't want to force it.

I just want to surrender. To let life take its course. To believe that one day, all of this—every joy, every ache, every goodbye—will make sense.

And for now, I choose to love him in the only way I still can: With the borrowed words of Rumi, which hold the weight of everything I feel:

"I choose to love him in silence, where I face no rejection. I choose to love him in loneliness, where no one owns him but me. I choose to adore him from a distance, where the pain stays bearable. I choose to kiss him in the wind, where the wind is gentler than my lips. I choose to hold him in my dreams, where in my dreams, he has no end."

And one last from me: *"I choose to love him, and I always will..."*

✦ ✦ ✦

"We were a story unfinished, not because we lacked love, but because we lacked words."

Chapter 16

What I Thought It Meant

*"Sometimes the heart clings to gestures the mind can't
make sense of—because when love feels unfinished,
even the smallest spark can look like a sign."*

It had been a few months since F ended everything. No texts. No
calls. Just silence. The kind of silence that doesn't just fill the air—
it crawls into your chest and makes a home out of your ribs. It felt
strange, almost cruel, to go from sharing our days—good mornings,
good nights, and everything in between—to nothing at all. Like someone had flipped a switch, and the light of my life was suddenly gone.

I felt hollow. Disoriented. I was still in love with him, and I didn't
know what to do with that love except hold it tightly and let it ache
quietly inside me.

I was grieving. Not just the end of a relationship, but the loss of
my best friend, my safe space, my person. I was trying to make sense
of the loneliness, the emptiness, the grief that gripped my chest every
day. Even now, as I write this, I still feel it—that flutter. That ache
disguised as butterflies. The kind you get when love refuses to leave,
even after the person has.

It's strange, isn't it? How something can hurt and still feel beautiful at the same time. I still smile through the pain, because love doesn't
just vanish. And neither do the memories.

I think about the morning we first met on New Year's, when everything felt new and possible. I think about our first kiss—how the world seemed to hold its breath in that moment. I see his smile, the one that always made me forget every worry, every shadow, every doubt. I remember the nights we spent curled up watching TV, the quiet comfort of simply being next to him, no words needed.

And then there are the bigger moments, like our magic trip to Disney World, when life felt lighter, brighter, as if the universe itself wanted us to believe in fairy tales.

All of them—and more. Every laugh, every fight, every silence that still carried meaning. I cherish them all. Because they were ours. No matter how much they hurt now, they were real. And nothing can take that away. They will always live inside me, like soft echoes of a love I'll never forget. These memories are stitched into me, and no matter how much time passes, they rise to the surface when I least expect it.

And then, just like that, the past reached for me again. It was mid-October when his name lit up on my phone.

My heart stopped. Just seeing those letters—his name—was enough to make my breath hitch and my hands tremble. In that instant, hope broke through the cracks like sunlight, uninvited and overwhelming. I smiled before I could stop myself. But the joy was quickly chased by fear. What if it was nothing? What if it was kindness laced with distance? What if this was the closure he needed—the closure I wasn't ready to give? What if the text wasn't a beginning, but the end dressed in softer words?

Still, I couldn't wait. My heart had already leapt ahead, pulling me toward him, reckless and desperate, as if love itself had written the message before I even read it.

I opened the message. *I'm in New York with my mom.*

I blinked at the screen, my heart skipping. *You're here?* I typed back, my fingers trembling. *Yeah… I was thinking maybe we could meet.*

For a second, I just stared. My chest tightened, my pulse quickened, and the room around me seemed to blur. I read the words over and over, like I was afraid they might disappear if I looked away. It felt unreal—after all the silence, after all the nights I had convinced myself I was nothing more than a memory to him, here he was, back in my city. Back in reach.

A thousand thoughts flooded me at once. Would seeing him heal me—or break me all over again? Would his eyes still look at me the way they once did, or would I find only distance staring back? Was this fate handing me another chance, or was it just a reminder that love, no matter how deep, can't always stay?

And yet, beneath the swirl of doubt and fear, hope pressed its way to the surface. Quiet, fragile, but undeniable. The possibility of seeing him again was enough to make me feel alive in a way I hadn't in months.

So I typed the only thing I could, the truth that had been waiting on my tongue since the day we last said goodbye: *You want to see me? When?*

I froze. Stunned. Why now? Why this? My mind spun with questions I couldn't stop: Did this mean something? Did he want to get back together? Was this his way of reaching for me again?

And yet—beneath the confusion, beneath the ache—a flicker of hope rose like it always did with him. Why else would he want me to meet his mom if he didn't care? If he didn't still feel something?

Of course, I said yes. I would've said yes to anything that meant seeing him again.

Because the truth was—I missed him so deeply it hurt. I missed the sound of his voice, the curve of his smile, the way being near him steadied me and unraveled me all at once. Even if it was only for a minute, even if it broke me later, I needed to feel close to him again.

After the breakup, I started learning Spanish. I can't even fully explain why. Maybe I thought if I could speak his language, he'd see me differently. Maybe he'd be proud of me. Maybe he'd love me again. I was so desperate to feel seen, to be chosen. I was willing to do anything.

I practiced my broken Spanish, rehearsing little phrases, imagining impressing his mom. I imagined her seeing me and thinking, *He's good for you.* I imagined that being enough to bring him back. I wanted to show that I cared, that I was worth it. That I belonged.

The evening finally came. I cleaned my apartment obsessively, cooked, prepared snacks, and nervously watched the clock. My phone buzzed again. *Come downstairs. We're waiting.*

Do you want to come up for a minute? I asked.

There was a pause. Then his reply: *No… we're heading out. I want to show my mom Times Square. Come with us.*

I stared at the screen, feeling that tiny sting of rejection. Why not upstairs? Why not just a few minutes alone? Still, the pull of him was stronger than the doubt. *Okay. I'll come down.*

None of that mattered. I just wanted to see him.

When I finally did, my breath caught in my throat. It was surreal, like walking back into a dream I thought I had lost forever. To see him standing there, alive in front of me after all the distance and silence—it was almost too much to take in. He felt like home and heartbreak all at once, the safest place and the sharpest wound colliding inside my chest.

We hugged, and in that moment, it was as if my heart was trying to stitch itself back together, thread by thread, right there in his arms. The familiar warmth of him, the scent I remembered without even knowing I'd memorized it, the way he held me just long enough to remind me that what we had was real—all of it came rushing back.

His mom was everything I had imagined and more—warm, sweet, gracious in a way that instantly softened the space around her. She carried herself with kindness that didn't need translation. We didn't say much—the language barrier was real, and I stumbled through my broken Spanish while she smiled through her careful English. But somehow, we understood each other anyway.

It wasn't just words that bridged the gap—it was the small gestures, the way she touched my arm when she laughed, the glances exchanged with her son that spoke of pride and love. It was the patience we gave each other, the willingness to meet halfway. With the mix of Spanish and English, with F translating here and there, with his friend jumping in to help—it all somehow worked. And in those moments, I realized that connection doesn't always need perfect words. Sometimes, presence alone is enough.

We walked together toward Times Square, the city buzzing around us with its usual restless energy. Neon lights flickered overhead, advertisements shouting from every corner, the hum of traffic and the shuffle of tourists filling the air. His friend chatted easily with his mom, their voices a gentle backdrop, while I walked silently beside him. Inches apart, yet miles away. The space between us felt charged—like there was a world of things unsaid hanging heavy in the air.

Every now and then our arms brushed as we walked, and each time, it felt like a spark I tried to hide inside my chest. He turned to me once, smiling in that way he always had—effortless, unguarded, devastating. For a moment, it was as if no time had passed, as if the distance, the silence, the heartbreak, had all been erased in the simple act of walking side by side again.

He hugged me once more, pulling me into him, and in that instant I was whole again. My heart recognized him before my mind could catch up, and I clung to the warmth of his body like it could anchor me to something real. I tried to soak up every detail: the sound of his voice when he leaned close to say something only I could hear, the way his laugh still curled at the edges like sunlight, the familiar comfort of simply being near him. I knew—even as I was living it—that this moment was fleeting. But I didn't care. I needed it. Even if it was borrowed.

When they walked me back to my apartment, my heart beat louder with every step, knowing our time was slipping through my fingers. On the stoop, just before we said goodbye, he looked at me and said he'd be returning to New York in two weeks for Halloween. *Maybe we could see each other again.*

Those words cracked something open inside me. Hope surged like wildfire, reckless and uncontainable. Maybe he missed me, too. Maybe this meant something—that I wasn't just a ghost from his past, that there was still a corner of his world where I belonged.

We said goodbye, and I stood frozen on the front stoop, watching him walk away—again. I prayed silently, desperately, that he would turn back. That just once, he would give me that last look over his shoulder, a sign that he still felt the pull too. But he didn't. He kept walking, step by step, until the city swallowed him whole.

The joy of that night dissolved into grief almost as quickly as it had come, leaving me hollow in its wake. And yet, I held onto it with both hands, clutching it like a fragile promise, even if it wasn't one. Because when you're still in love with someone who has already let you go, even the smallest sliver of hope can feel like a lifeline.

But this time, I had something to hold onto. Hope. The kind that kept me awake at night, spinning possibilities, imagining what it might feel like to be chosen, to be wanted again. Hope that maybe, just maybe, Halloween would bring us another chance.

Halloween was coming. And a part of me still believed—foolishly, stubbornly—that maybe that night would bring him back to me.

✦ ✦ ✦

"Sometimes the heart clings to gestures the mind can't make sense of—because when love feels unfinished, even the smallest spark can look like a sign."

Chapter 17

Dressed in Hope, Left in Silence

"Sometimes the silence after hope is louder than any goodbye."

Two weeks later, Halloween arrived—and with it, all the hope I had wrapped around that night like a costume. I had no idea how to dress—not just physically, but emotionally. I was terrified and excited, anxious and romantic. I wanted to believe this could be the beginning of something new. That maybe all the pain had finally led us back to each other.

I chose an outfit that made me feel confident—plaid shirt, fitted jeans, and boots. A little rugged, a little playful. Dressed like a lumberjack, but in a way that felt intentional, almost like armor. It wasn't about trying to look perfect; it was about showing up as myself, solid and grounded, even if inside I was anything but.

I added just enough makeup to feel pretty—enough to catch a little light on my face, enough to remind myself I was still attractive, still worth seeing—but not so much that it felt like pretending. I didn't want to look like I was performing for him. I wanted to look like me.

As I stood in front of the mirror, I whispered silent reassurances: *"This night will be fun. Light. Maybe even healing."* I told myself he wanted to see me—that had to mean something. That maybe this wasn't just a casual meet-up, but a sign. A chance. The smallest flicker of possibility that not everything between us was gone.

And I held on to that thought like it was oxygen.

It was one of the biggest Halloween parties around—hundreds, maybe thousands of people, all dressed to impress. A parade of costumes and masks, laughter echoing through the streets. The mystery of it all felt magical. I was there with friends, and we were having a great time—dancing, admiring the costumes, caught in the electric energy of the night. It was all so alive, so vibrant. I was genuinely happy for a while, caught in the magic.

But still, my eyes kept scanning the crowd. Every flash of color, every costume that passed by—I searched for him in all of it. I knew F was out there somewhere. My chest tightened with every second that went by, my mind spinning with the same question over and over: *What costume did he choose?* I couldn't stop wondering, couldn't stop picturing it, couldn't stop needing to see him.

And then—there he was.

First, a familiar face broke through the blur of strangers: one of his friends, smiling as if he knew something I didn't. Then another. They were dressed like characters from *Aladdin,* their costumes playful, bright, almost too perfect for the night. And behind them… him.

F.

The sight of him hit me harder than I expected, like the air had been punched out of my lungs. My eyes locked on him, drinking in the details—the way the costume fit him, the way he carried himself, the way he seemed to glow just by existing in the same space as me. For a moment, the noise of the party, the music, the laughter—all of it blurred. It was just him. Just us.

And in that instant, all I wanted was to close the distance between us, to step into whatever role this night had written for us—even if it was only for a moment. I couldn't stop smiling. My heart leapt in my chest like it was trying to reach him before I could.

But as they approached, I felt it. A shift. Something invisible but undeniable. His hug was quick, cold, mechanical—like checking off a box on a list. He said hello, but it felt like a stranger's voice. No warmth. No spark. No trace of the man who once held me like I was everything he wanted. His eyes slid past mine too quickly, his smile too thin to be real.

And just as suddenly as he appeared, he was gone again—swallowed by the crowd, swept away with his friends in a blur of costumes and laughter that didn't include me.

I stood frozen, my smile collapsing, trying to make sense of what had just happened. Two weeks ago, things had felt so different—so full of hope. We had spoken. We had shared words that carried weight. I had let myself believe again.

What changed?

Was it me?

Did I say something wrong? Did I do something that pushed him away again?

The questions circled me like vultures, and I had no answers—only the hollow echo of his absence where warmth should have been.

I had to know. I left my friends and wandered through the crowd, scanning faces, looking for him. Eventually, I spotted his group. Some I knew from New York, others he had brought from Orlando. I approached, trying to act normal, pretending my heart wasn't in my throat.

His friends were kind, welcoming. The ones I knew introduced me to the rest. I chatted with them for a bit, but I barely heard what anyone was saying. My eyes were on him.

F was distant. Detached.

He stood to the side, barely acknowledging me, as if my presence was an inconvenience he couldn't quite ignore but didn't want to engage with either.

He didn't look at me. Didn't speak to me.

It was like I wasn't even there.

And every time I inched closer, hoping for some flicker of warmth, some sign that he still saw me, he drifted further away—like I was chasing a shadow that kept dissolving in the dark, as if my nearness was something to avoid. Like *I* was something to avoid.

He couldn't even meet my eyes. And that—God, that—was the part that gutted me.

And I didn't understand why. I didn't know what had shifted between the last time he held me and this moment where he could barely stand near me.

I was drowning in questions I couldn't ask, swallowing them down because I already feared the answers.

I stood there, surrounded by a sea of strangers and flashing lights, yet the loudest thing in the night was the silence between us. He was right in front of me, but emotionally, he was a million miles away.

I was invisible to the person I had once loved more than anyone. The person whose attention used to feel like sunlight now made me feel like I was standing in the cold.

I tried to hold it together. I smiled. I stayed polite. I tried not to let the tremor in my chest spill into my voice.

But inside, I was breaking—splintering in ways I didn't think anyone could recover from. I was breaking apart so violently it was hard to breathe.

The pain wasn't just emotional—it was physical, sharp and hollow all at once, like someone had reached into my chest and ripped out my heart with bare hands, leaving an aching hollow that nothing could fill.

In that moment, I wasn't just losing him. I was losing the version of myself that still believed he cared.

And that was the part that hurt the most.

The truth hit me harder than the breakup ever had—because at least then, I had words. This time, I had nothing but his silence, and it screamed louder than anything he could have said.

Just silence.

I kept asking myself over and over: *Why?* What did I do? Why was he so cold? Why couldn't he even look at me?

I walked home from that party completely shattered. Not because he said anything cruel. Not because we fought.

But because his silence screamed the truth louder than words ever could, because he did nothing. Because nothing was worse. Because nothing meant he didn't care.

And when someone you love stops caring, there's no coming back from that.

He didn't want me anymore. And it broke me.

But it also woke me up.

Because love—real love—doesn't make you feel invisible. It doesn't make you beg for scraps of affection. It doesn't vanish when things get hard.

The night I had clung to as a beacon of hope had turned into a nightmare. I lay awake, waiting for a message. An explanation. Anything.

But my phone never lit up. Not that night. Not the next. Not ever.

And I couldn't bring myself to text him. How could I? How could I reach out to someone who couldn't even meet my eyes?

In that moment, I knew—it was over. Not just the relationship. But the hope. The dream. The version of myself that kept waiting for him to love me the way I loved him.

That Halloween night wasn't just the end of us. It felt like the end of me, because that night, I realized something I didn't want to see:

He didn't come to find me. He didn't try to talk to me. He didn't care how I felt.

And I had to stop pretending that he did.

✦ ✦ ✦

"I wandered through the night dressed in hope, but his silence was louder than the music, sharper than the cold. And in that quiet ache, I learned—some goodbyes are spoken with eyes that refuse to meet yours."

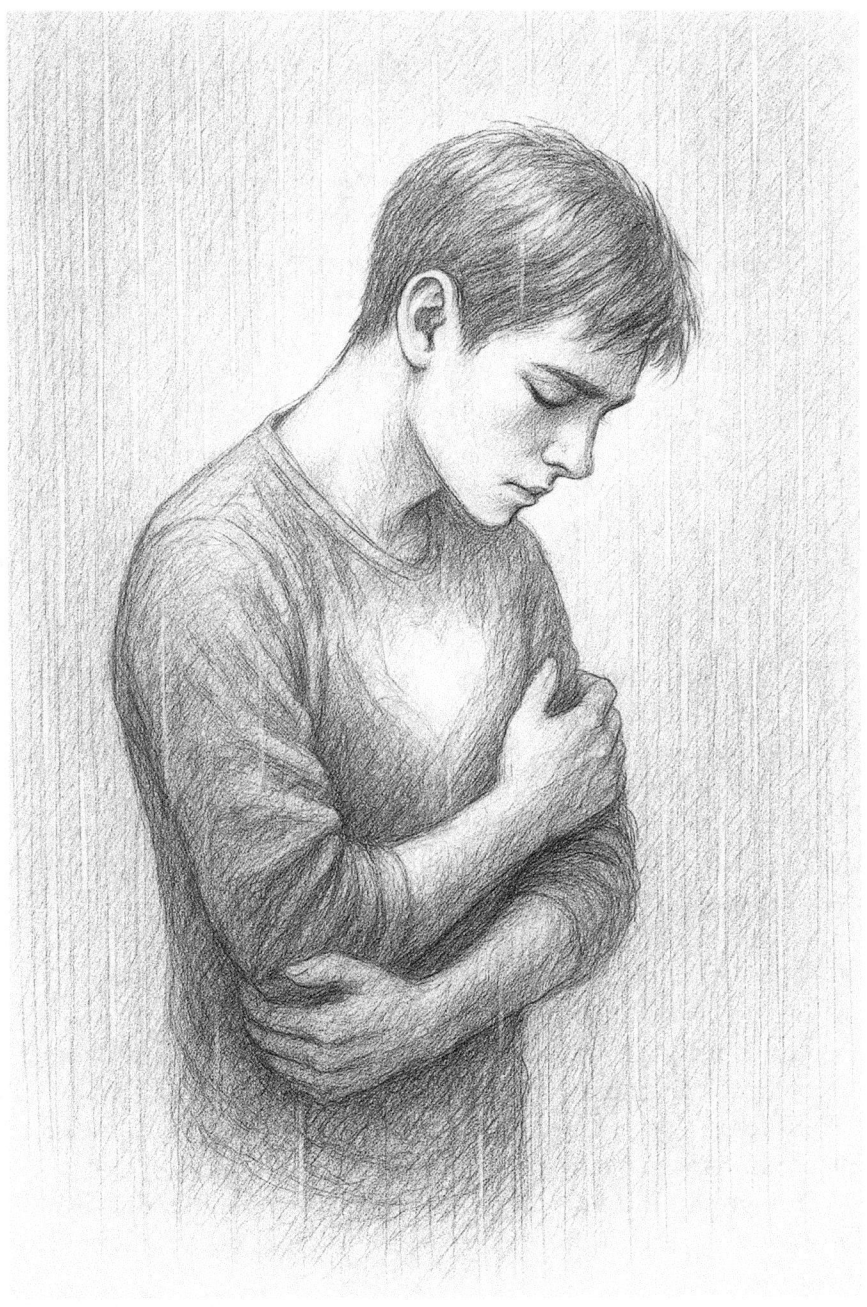

Chapter 18

The Days After – Grieving Someone Still Alive

*"Sometimes the loudest heartbreak isn't in the words
spoken, but in the silence that follows them."*

The morning after Halloween, I woke up still wearing last night's makeup and a heart that felt too heavy to carry.

My phone was silent. No missed calls. No messages. Just a black screen that mirrored the void inside me.

I laid there for hours, unable to move, barely able to breathe. I kept replaying the night over and over again—the hug, the coldness in his eyes, the way he avoided me like I was a stranger.

I asked myself the same questions on a loop:

Why? What changed? What did I do?

But no answer came.

And somehow, that silence hurt more than anything he could've said.

Because silence has a way of saying everything.

Words can be softened, bent, dressed up in kindness. But silence? Silence is sharp. It cuts without warning, without mercy.

It lingers in the air, filling every space where love used to live. It forces you to create your own answers—most of them crueler than the truth.

His silence told me I wasn't worth the effort of an explanation. It told me he'd already moved on, already given the words I wanted to someone else. It told me I was no longer someone to choose, only someone to avoid.

And the worst part?

Silence echoes.

Even after he walked away, I could still hear it—ringing louder than anything he could have ever said.

I didn't know how to grieve someone who was still alive.

Someone who might have been laughing that morning, drinking coffee, moving on. Someone who just days before had hugged me like maybe something was still there. Someone who had told me he would see me again.

I kept thinking: *How do you let go of someone who's still out there, walking around in the world like you never existed?*

It was a strange kind of heartbreak. Not sharp and loud—but slow and dull. Like a bruise spreading across my chest, growing darker every hour.

I didn't cry right away. I felt too numb to cry. Too stunned. The pain sat just beneath my skin, quietly pulsing, waiting for permission to rise.

I went through the motions: showered, got dressed, answered texts I didn't care about. I smiled at people who asked how my night went and said, *"It was fun,"* even though it was the night I shattered.

But behind the mask, I was breaking.

No one tells you how lonely it feels to love someone who's already gone. How disorienting it is to realize you were holding on to a version of a person they no longer are. Or maybe never were.

The days after Halloween felt like walking through a fog.

I kept hoping—maybe he'd text. Maybe he'd explain. Maybe this was all a mistake.

But deep down, I knew. I knew he had already made his choice. I just hadn't made mine yet.

I still had so much love inside me. And no place to put it.

I kept replaying memories—soft ones, beautiful ones. The way he used to look at me. The way we laughed in the car. The way I used to feel safe with him.

And the question that haunted me most was:

Did he ever feel it too? Or was I the only one who thought it was real?

That question nearly destroyed me.

Because to believe it wasn't real meant everything I had felt, everything I had given, was one-sided. And that kind of realization cracks something deeper than the heart. It touches the soul.

And yet, somewhere in all that grief, I felt something else stirring. Not hope. Not yet.

But clarity.

A small voice inside me—quiet but steady—began to whisper:

You didn't imagine it. You loved deeply. Honestly. Fully. And that means something—even if he couldn't hold it.

Grieving someone who's still alive means mourning the version of yourself you were when you believed you were loved.

It means letting go of the future you thought you were building. And it means accepting that closure might never come from them—it has to come from within you.

I didn't find peace that week. Or even strength.

But I did find the truth.

And maybe that's where real healing begins.

✦ ✦ ✦

"Grieving someone still alive is the cruelest kind of goodbye—because they go on living while you quietly learn how to survive their absence."

Chapter 19

The Ghost Season

"Healing doesn't always look like freedom—it often looks like surviving the silence long enough to hear your own voice again."

Somewhere between grief and letting go, there's a season no one talks about.

It's not the crying-on-the-bathroom-floor kind of pain. That part has passed. The sobs have quieted. The sharpness has dulled.

But the ache— The ache lingers.

It's quieter now. Emptier.

It's the ghost season—the time when someone is gone, but still everywhere. When their absence takes up more space than their presence ever did. When memories stop screaming and start whispering—and somehow, that's worse.

His name doesn't make my chest cave in anymore, but it still pulls at something deep inside me. Something soft. Something tired.

I wasn't drowning anymore, but I wasn't breathing freely either.

That's where I lived for a while. In the in-between. Not broken, but not whole. Not moving on, but no longer holding on.

It's a strange kind of limbo—where the world keeps turning, but your heart hasn't caught up.

The days grew colder. November arrived like a slow ache.

I went to work. I smiled. I showed up. I met with friends and asked them how they were, carefully avoiding their eyes when they asked the same. I replied to emails. I even laughed at the right moments.

And from the outside, I looked okay.

But underneath it all, I was haunted. Not just by him—but by the version of myself that existed when he loved me. Or when I thought he did.

That version of me… he was softer. Hopeful. He believed in magic, in timing, in second chances. He believed that love meant staying.

I missed him. I missed the way I used to feel in his arms—like I belonged. Like maybe, for once, I wouldn't be left.

Every little thing reminded me of him. A song in a coffee shop. A coat like his on a stranger. A street corner. A pair of eyes that almost looked like his. A text I typed but never sent.

He was gone—but he was everywhere.

That's the cruelty of heartbreak—it teaches you how deeply someone can root themselves in your life without ever really choosing to stay.

I kept asking myself, *When does it stop? When do I stop replaying every moment? When do I stop hoping he'll come back?*

But the truth is… part of me didn't want it to stop. Because if it stopped, it meant the story was really over. It meant I'd have to accept that he wasn't coming back.

That the apology I held out for—the explanation, the understanding, the closure—I was never going to get it. And maybe even worse… maybe he didn't think I deserved it.

That's what broke me the most. Not just the loss of him—but the loss of certainty.

The loss of the belief that love, once real, was unbreakable. That if someone truly saw your soul—if he kissed it, touched it, held it close—he wouldn't walk away from it. I thought love meant safety. I thought if I gave him every part of me, he would treasure it, protect it, keep it. I thought he would.

But he didn't.

And that's when the questions began.

I started questioning everything. My worth. My memories. My judgment.

Had I made it all up? Did I imagine the way he looked at me, the way his eyes softened when they met mine? Did I hallucinate the way his arms held me like home? Did I dream up the moments when the world felt like it only belonged to us?

Had he ever really loved me at all? Or had I been clinging to scraps and calling them love?

Was I too much for him? Not enough for him? Both?

Or was I just the fool—writing a love story in stone while he was sketching his part in sand, ready for the tide to wash it away the second it got inconvenient?

I hated it. I hated how much space he still took up in my head, as if he had moved out of my life but left his ghost behind to torment me. I hated that I still checked my phone like it owed me salvation, like one text from him could resurrect me. I hated how a single name—his name—could pull me back into the ruins of us, undoing weeks of pretending I was okay.

I hated who I had become because of him. Smaller. Weaker. A version of myself I didn't even recognize anymore.

But the worst part? I didn't know how to take my power back.

It felt like he had taken it with him the moment he walked away. Like he slipped it into his pocket without even noticing, and I was left behind—empty, desperate, waiting for someone who wasn't coming back to hand me back pieces of myself he probably never even realized he was carrying.

And that's what gutted me most of all. Not that he left— but that I let him take me with him when he did.

Some days I felt strong. I'd whisper to myself, *"You deserve more than this silence. You deserve more than someone who made you feel hard to love."*

And sometimes, I almost believed it. I'd straighten my back, inhale like the air itself could fill the emptiness he left, and convince myself I was done reaching for someone who had already let me fall.

But other days... I came undone. I'd sit in the dim light of my room, staring at my phone like it was a lifeline, scrolling through old messages until the words blurred and my chest burned. I reread them as if the meaning might change this time, as if one hidden truth would leap out and tell me I hadn't imagined it all. *Where did it go wrong? What did I do? What did I miss?*

I counted the days since we last spoke like I was waiting for an expiration date on my grief. But the date never came. Instead, each morning I woke up heavier than the last, my body carrying the silence like an anchor.

Healing didn't look like clarity. It didn't look like relief. It looked like survival.

It looked like quiet persistence— like dragging myself out of bed even when my body begged me to stay down. Like forcing myself to eat when food tasted like ash in my mouth. Like waking up and making the brutal choice not to text him, even when my hands shook with the urge. Like walking past the restaurant where we had our date and keeping my eyes fixed straight ahead, muscles stiff, fighting the instinct to turn, to search, to hope. Like deleting his photos one by one, my hands trembling, my throat tight, my stomach hollow, like I was burying him in pieces I'd never dig back up.

It was grief without ceremony. Letting go without permission.

And it was brutal. Because no one teaches you how to mourn someone who's still alive. How to bury a love that still breathes somewhere out there without you. How to carry the weight of absence that still pulses like a heartbeat.

My body carried it all. The sleepless nights, staring at the ceiling until the sun crept through the blinds. The knots in my stomach that made me skip meals. The constant fatigue, like grief had settled into my bones, making everything heavier, slower, harder. The hollow ache in my chest that no amount of sleep could fix.

I looked in the mirror and didn't recognize myself—eyes tired, face drawn, the spark I used to have dimmed into something duller, more fragile.

But slowly—imperceptibly—something shifted.

The sadness began to feel less sharp, like a bruise instead of a blade. The silence lost some of its echo. And beneath it, in the cracks of the quiet, I began to hear something else—

My own voice. My own needs. My own worth.

It was faint. Wobbly. But it was there.

And maybe that's what healing really is— Not the dramatic moment of closure. Not a sudden, cinematic peace. But the quiet, trembling decision to keep choosing yourself… even when your body still aches for him.

I wasn't over him. But for the first time, I wasn't trying to be.

I wasn't begging the pain to leave. I wasn't clinging to the hope that he'd come back. I was just learning how to live again.

Without him. For me.

Silence can break you in ways words never could. And when I was at my quietest, that's when the wrong kind of voice found me.

"The ghost season doesn't end when the memories fade—it ends when you finally remember that your own presence is enough."

Chapter 20

Crypto, Catfish, and the Cost of Loneliness

"Shame thrives in silence. But when you
speak it, you take its power away."

I don't even know how to begin this chapter of my life, but I know I have to. Because the shame I carry isn't mine to carry alone. And if there's one person out there who reads this and feels a little less alone in their own heartbreak, then maybe this pain can mean something more than just loss.

A few months after Halloween heartbreak, I met someone on Tinder. His name was Felix.

It started like most conversations do nowadays—casual, light-hearted, a few jokes, a few shared photos. But it didn't take long before we were texting every day. There was something about him that made me feel safe. Warm. Heard. I found myself smiling at my phone again, waiting for his name to pop up. We talked about our dreams, our pasts, our futures. He made me laugh. He asked questions no one else bothered to ask. For the first time in what felt like forever, I felt seen.

And that's why I need to tell this story—because people assume you get scammed because you're stupid, or careless, or greedy. But that's not what happened. I was just… empty. And he filled that emptiness with attention and tenderness and hope.

You see, I never really got over F. I wasn't talking about him anymore, but I thought about him every single day. I carried that heartbreak like a ghost on my back. I truly believed I'd never love again. I was just existing. Going through the motions. And then Felix appeared, and I thought, maybe... maybe this is it. Maybe I finally get to feel something good.

He didn't rush me. He didn't pressure me. He just showed up, every day. And when you've been abandoned, overlooked, or replaced like I had been—consistency feels like love. And I craved it.

A few weeks into our conversations, he started talking about the future. Not our future, exactly—more like the future in general. He told me I should think about retirement, investing, real estate. He said he owned a few apartments in Miami and invested in crypto. If I wanted, he'd show me how. No pressure.

And to be honest, it didn't even feel like manipulation. It felt like someone caring. Guiding. Trying to help. I had been so careless with money before, forced to drain my savings just to survive the last few years. Maybe this was my chance to rebuild.

He helped me set up a Coinbase account and a Trust Wallet. Walked me through everything. He never asked for my passwords—I did it all myself. It felt safe. Secure. Like I was finally in control of something.

I started small. I invested $1,000. I made $100. Then $200. He sent me screenshots of his own success—$20,000 in a single night. He made it look so easy. So doable.

So I added more. $20,000. I made $2,000. Then $4,000.

He kept saying, *"If you can get to $100,000, you could be making $30–40K this month."* He said he just put in $80K himself.

I didn't have that kind of money. But he suggested a personal loan. Said I'd make it back and pay it off quickly. I thought, why not? This is my shot.

I borrowed $50,000. I even pulled money from my IRA.

In total, I put in $100,000. Half borrowed. Half mine.

And it was working. Or at least, it looked like it was. I was "earning" thousands in returns. We kept texting every day. We even started planning to meet—he said he lived in Miami, and I booked my flight.

Then, three days before I was supposed to fly out, he said his uncle got sick and he had to go take care of him. He sent photos of his dog, updates from the hospital. I believed him. Why wouldn't I? He had never given me a reason not to.

And then everything changed.

I was scrolling Facebook one night when a mutual friend posted a photo of *"Felix"*—with the caption:

"We lost another soul. Rest in peace, my dear friend."

I froze.

I had just spoken to him.

I clicked on the profile, confused. And there it was—the truth. The man in the photo had died by suicide days earlier.

Felix had stolen his identity. Used his photos. His life. His face.

I had been catfished. For over three months.

I confronted him immediately. And he admitted it.

He told me he did it because he thought he was ugly. That I'd never talk to him if I knew what he really looked like. But everything else, he said, was *"real."*

And maybe part of me wanted to believe that. But my bank account told a different story.

I tried to withdraw my money. I followed the same steps he had shown me before. But now—suddenly—nothing worked. The money was there, but I couldn't access it. Frozen.

I contacted support. I sent screenshots, account info, everything.

Days later, they responded.

I had been scammed.

All the "trades"? Fake. All the earnings? Illusions.

Everything was gone.

My savings. My emergency fund. My retirement. Gone.

And I was $50,000 in debt. That was the beginning of my financial struggle.

And the worst part? The shame.

Not just for losing the money. But for wanting love so badly... that I believed it.

I believed in him. I believed I was finally getting my life together. I believed I was worthy of something good.

But it was all a lie.

And still, I can't bring myself to hate him. Not fully. Because that would mean hating the version of myself that trusted. That hoped. That needed so desperately to feel loved.

He didn't just scam my bank account. He scammed my heart. And that's the wound I don't know how to heal yet.

So here I am—broke, grieving, humiliated.

But somehow, still breathing.

Still writing.

Still trying to believe that not all love will end like this.

I may have been fooled. But I wasn't weak. I was just human.

I just wanted to be seen. To be chosen. To matter.

And that's not something I'll ever be ashamed of again.

✦ ✦ ✦

"You can lose money, you can lose love, but you never lose the worth of your own heart."

Chapter 21

When Hope Becomes a Weapon

"Sometimes, the need to be loved is so deep, it makes us believe even the most convincing lies."

At the time, I thought I had nothing left to lose. Still grieving F. Still carrying the echo of a love that never healed. I was doing everything I could to forget—everything I could to stop thinking about him. I wasn't moving on, I was just trying to survive the silence.

And that's why it hurts to write this.

Because I wasn't just catfished. I was emotionally groomed. I was scammed—financially, but also spiritually.

Felix didn't find me at my best. He found me at my lowest. And he used that loneliness as currency.

In the days after everything came crashing down, I was numb. Not angry. Not even devastated—just hollow. Like I had given so much of myself away that there was nothing left to feel with.

I couldn't eat. I couldn't sleep. I kept refreshing my Trust Wallet as if staring at frozen numbers would somehow bring them back. I walked around my apartment in silence, ashamed to tell anyone what had happened. Ashamed that I had been so easily deceived. Ashamed that I still missed him.

Because even after everything… I missed the version of him that never existed.

But grief is strange like that. You don't just grieve the money or the betrayal—you grieve the future you thought you were walking into. The conversations that felt real. The comfort of being chosen. The lie that made you feel loved, even if only for a moment.

And the truth is, I didn't get scammed because I was careless. I got scammed because I was grieving.

When Felix came into my life, I was already in pieces. I was still reeling from losing F—still carrying a quiet, unspoken ache that lived in every part of my day. I didn't talk about him anymore, but he never really left my mind. I thought about him constantly. I was doing everything I could to forget—everything I could to move on—but I wasn't okay. I was just pretending.

I was still heartbroken. Still shattered by the way things ended. Still waiting for someone, anyone, to make me feel like I mattered again.

And then came Felix. Kind, consistent, attentive. He made me laugh again. He gave me something to look forward to. He made me feel seen. Understood. Wanted.

And when you've been living with silent grief—grief no one can see—being wanted feels like oxygen.

So yes, I was vulnerable. Maybe more than I'd ever been in my life. I was so desperate to feel loved again that I clung to the first person who offered it. I ignored the red flags because I wanted to believe. I needed to believe. I had to believe there was still goodness out there.

He didn't just find me at a low point—he found me at rock bottom. And he gave me something that looked like hope. That felt like love.

But it wasn't.

It was a performance. A trap.

And once the mask came off and the money disappeared, I was left sitting in the wreckage—not just of a financial scam, but of my own broken heart all over again.

And slowly, I began to understand that I wasn't stupid. I was starving.

Starving to be seen. To be valued. To finally feel like I wasn't disposable.

Felix didn't create that need in me—he found it, and he fed it, and then he used it against me.

But this is where the story shifts.

Because even in the wreckage—even in the silence after the truth—I was still here. I was still breathing. I was still mine.

So I began to rebuild. Not with grand gestures, but with small acts of defiance.

I talked. First to a friend. Then another. And then I wrote this. Each time, the shame grew smaller. Each time, I felt a little less alone.

I got back into therapy. I journaled like my life depended on it—because in a way, it did.

I stopped asking, *"How could I fall for this?"* and started asking, *"What was I missing that made me so desperate to believe?"*

And the answer was always the same: I was in pain. I was grieving. I was still bleeding from a love I had never truly let go of.

And that doesn't make me weak. That makes me human.

I also began to rebuild my trust—in myself. Because the cruelest part of being scammed isn't just losing your money. It's losing your confidence. It's no longer trusting your instincts, your judgment, your worth.

So I started small. I said no. I drew boundaries. I honored my feelings, even when they didn't make sense to anyone else. I stopped reaching for the next person to save me. And started learning how to save myself.

Emotionally, it's still a climb. There are days I feel fine. And days I feel like I'm drowning again.

But the difference now? I know I'm going to survive.

And maybe that's what healing really is— Not pretending the cracks don't exist, But learning to live with them wide open, And still believing you deserve to be loved.

Not because someone finally chose you. But because you finally chose yourself.

✦ ✦ ✦

"Sometimes survival isn't loud. Sometimes it's the quiet decision to keep going, one fragile day at a time."

Chapter 22

When It All Made Sense

*"Sometimes, the silence holds the answers
we've been begging for all along."*

The time passed. Some days felt longer. Some felt like minutes. I was still trying to put myself together after everything ended with F. I was broken—shattered into pieces—and I kept reaching down, trying to gather them all, trying to make myself whole again.

Some days were easier. Others dragged me straight back into the pit—the hole of grief, of sadness, of questions that had no answers. Not a single day went by without thinking about him. Sometimes it was a fleeting memory, a flash of his laugh. Other times, it consumed me. I lived in the past, searching for closure that never came. Because when you don't have closure, you make up a million endings in your head. And none of them bring peace.

I kept myself busy. I tried. Because when your mind is occupied, you don't have space to fall apart. I was functioning—until the sun went down. Evenings were my undoing. When the noise faded and the world got quiet, the thoughts got louder. Sharper. More painful.

I didn't know how to sit with the pain. I didn't know how to let my heart breathe. I was a mess—emotionally, mentally, physically. I partied. I went out. I filled the empty spaces with anything I could—music, noise, people, food. Late at night, I found comfort in ice cream, pizza, and chocolate—tiny pleasures I used as Band-Aids for the hole he left.

One day, I ended up at a party. And yes, it was fun. I laughed. I danced. I used drugs to feel lighter. We all wanted to escape—my friends and I. Everyone was carrying something they didn't know how to name, a heaviness that clung to us in silence. Some carried heartbreak, some regret, others just the dull ache of feeling stuck in lives that didn't feel like their own. None of us said it out loud, but it lived in the way we moved, the way our laughter sometimes cracked at the edges. We just wanted one night—one night to forget, to dissolve into the music, into the crowd, into something bigger than the weight we carried. We just wanted to feel good, even if it was only for a few hours.

That night turned into a morning-after party at someone's apartment. Post-COVID, these house parties had become normal. People found ways to gather, to connect, to lose themselves in the blur of music and company.

I walked into the apartment. It was already Sunday morning. Light crept through the windows. Strangers lounged on couches and floors, not ready to go home. And then I saw a familiar face.

It was one of F's friends. The one from Orlando—the one he left me for that night after the party. The one who became living proof that I wasn't enough. That night, he chose him over me, and in an instant, I had gone from everything to nothing. Seeing him now was like reopening a wound I had convinced myself was healing.

My heart slammed in my chest. My throat tightened. A part of me wanted to turn away, to shield myself from what this meant. But another part—the desperate, reckless part—clung to the hope that this could only mean one thing. Was F here too? He had to be. Why else would his friend be here?

The thought electrified me. My body was restless, my hands shaking slightly as I looked around the room, scanning every face, every shadow. I searched for him like someone starving, like maybe his presence could feed something in me I had been starving of for months. One glimpse. One sign. Anything. Maybe tonight would be different. Maybe we'd finally lock eyes, and something unspoken would shatter the silence between us. Maybe he'd walk toward me instead of away.

But he wasn't there. The longer I looked, the emptier it felt. The noise of the party swelled around me, but inside, all I could hear was the hollow echo of absence. He wasn't here. Still, I couldn't stop searching, as if he might appear in the next second, as if my looking alone might summon him.

And when I finally gave up—when I tried to paste on a smile, to surrender myself back to the music and laughter—the question lingered like a knife pressed against my ribs: why is his friend here? Who does he know here? And why does the answer matter to me more than anything else?

I asked a few people. No one knew him. Not even the host. He was just there, drunk, slowly drifting into sleep on the couch in the middle of a room full of strangers. And I was the only one who knew his name.

I couldn't leave him like that. He meant something to F. And F still meant everything to me.

So I walked up to him.

"Hi, do you remember me?"

He looked up, eyes blurry, and said, *"Yes, I do."*

We talked a little. I offered him a place to rest. My apartment was nearby, and I figured he'd be more comfortable there. He agreed.

At my place, we ate something, then passed out from exhaustion. I gave him my bed while I stayed on the couch. Hours later, when we woke up, the fog had lifted. The alcohol and drugs were mostly gone from our systems. We started talking.

I asked why he was in New York. He told me he came with friends from Orlando for a birthday party. More were supposed to come—including F—but a snowstorm had canceled most of the flights. He was lucky; he took an earlier one.

And then I asked the question that had lived in me for months:

"How is F? Have you seen him lately? Is he okay?"

He smiled. *"He's great. We see each other a lot."*

He kept talking about their friend group, and then one name came up repeatedly—Sal.

So I asked, *"Who's Sal?"*

And casually, he said it.

"That's F's boyfriend."

My world stopped.

"He has a boyfriend? Since when?"

"Since July. They've been together for a while."

July. That was when everything fell apart between us.

The pieces I had worked so hard to hold together... fell again.

"Do you have a picture of him? Can I see?"

And he showed me. A photo of F and his boyfriend. Smiling. Together.

And that's when it all made sense...

That Halloween night. The distance. The coldness. The avoidance. His eyes not meeting mine. His hands not reaching for me. The nervous energy. The awkwardness. It wasn't random.

He was there... with his boyfriend.

And the person he chose—the boyfriend—wasn't some stranger I could file away in my mind as separate from me. No. He was one of the people I had met that night. One of the faces in the crowd I barely noticed, just another body moving through the noise and the music.

That made it worse. That made the silence louder. That made the pain sharper. It made the confusion feel cruel.

Because while I was scanning the room, wondering if F might come find me, he was already standing next to the person he wanted to be with.

And I was just a shadow of the past. A ghost in a room where he was building something new.

I sat there in silence after seeing that photo. It felt like something cracked open inside me—a wound that had never fully healed now torn wide again. But this time, there was no more wondering. No more hopeful excuses. No more maybes.

This was the truth. This was the closure I thought I wanted.

And still, it broke me.

I had imagined that moment so many times—running into him again, talking, maybe even hugging. Maybe one last kiss. Something soft. I never imagined it would come from a photo on someone else's phone. A truth delivered without warning, without gentleness.

He had a boyfriend. He had moved on. He had a whole new chapter.

And I was just a footnote.

The weird thing is—I wasn't even angry. I wanted to be. I wanted to feel rage, betrayal. Something sharp to hold onto. But what I felt was worse: I felt like nothing.

Like I had never mattered.

Like all the moments, the love, the fighting, the intimacy, the hope—I had imagined it all. Or maybe I had just loved him so loudly, so deeply, that I drowned out everything else.

I walked into the bathroom and stared at myself in the mirror.

And I didn't even cry.

Because there was nothing left to cry out. I had emptied myself long ago, crying over someone who had already let go. Someone who had quietly slipped out the back door of my heart and into someone else's arms.

But here's the most painful part:

Even after everything—even after the lies, the avoidance, the abandonment—I knew deep in my heart that he didn't mean to hurt me. He wasn't cruel. He wasn't evil.

He just didn't know how to tell me. In his own way, he was trying to protect me. Maybe he thought silence was kinder. Maybe he believed it was better to let me drift away without knowing. But the truth?

The truth hurts once. The lie hurts every day.

If only he had told me. Not so I could stop loving him. But so I could stop holding my breath.

Because that's what I'd been doing—holding my breath for months, waiting for a sign, a message, a clue. Anything to help me make sense of it all.

And now that I had it… I could finally exhale.

I didn't cry. Because there are wounds so deep they don't bleed anymore. They just sit inside you. Silent. Aching. Waiting for you to accept that they're part of you now.

And in that silence, I finally said goodbye.

Not the kind you speak out loud. The kind that happens in your bones. Quiet. Final. Heavy.

I never stopped loving him. I don't think I ever will. But I finally stopped waiting.

Love doesn't always end with a final kiss or a slammed door. Sometimes it ends in a quiet room, with a picture on a phone, with no one watching you break. Sometimes love ends not because it wasn't real—but because it wasn't right anymore. And even when you don't get the goodbye you deserved, you still have to find a way to say it to yourself.

He didn't owe me anything. He was free to love who he wanted, to move on, to find happiness—even if that happiness wasn't with me. He didn't do anything wrong.

He didn't have to hide him from me. He could have just been honest. I would've understood. It would've hurt—God, it would've hurt—but I would've understood. Because as much as I loved him, I always knew that you can't force love on someone who doesn't love you back. I would've walked away, at least with some answers. With some dignity. With a reason.

But instead, I walked away with silence. With pieces. With questions that haunted me in the quietest hours of the night.

So that's what I did.

In silence. In stillness. I let him go.

Not because I stopped loving him, but because I started loving myself enough to stop waiting.

✦ ✦ ✦

"Sometimes, the hardest truth isn't that they moved on—it's that you must too."

Chapter 23

What Was Left After Everything Ended

"Sometimes closure doesn't arrive with answers—it arrives with acceptance that the answers may never come."

Finally, I had my answer—some kind of closure about what happened between us. About what happened on that Halloween night. About why he didn't see me that night—or any day after. I had my closure... or so I told myself.

He had moved on. He was in a relationship now—not with me, but with someone else. Someone he chose. Someone he wanted. And not for lack of trying on my part. I had tried so hard. I gave everything I could—and I would've done it all again if I knew there was still a chance. But in that moment, I finally understood: there wasn't.

I had to close that chapter of my life. I had to forget. But do you ever really forget? No. You don't.

But I had to try. I had to live. I had to keep moving. Even when it felt lonely. Even when the sadness felt unbearable. Because if I stayed in that pain, I don't know if I would still be here now.

So I deleted every picture we had together. I packed away or hid anything that reminded me of him. And in a moment of pure grief, I smashed the Simba coffee mug he gave me—the one that meant everything to me. That mug held more than coffee; it held memories, moments, and the emotions I was still trying to survive.

I kept going. I unfollowed, muted, blocked—him, his friends, anything that might show his face or his life. Not because I hated him, but because I needed to breathe.

I wanted to delete his number. To block him completely. But I didn't. I couldn't. That would mean slamming the last door shut. Throwing away the final key. And I just couldn't do that.

Some part of me needed to leave that door slightly open. Just a crack. Just enough for a sliver of hope to slip through if the universe ever wanted it to.

Should I have shut it? Probably. I would have saved myself a lot of pain. But I couldn't burn the last bridge to the man I had loved more than anything.

Time passed. Slowly, painfully—but it passed.

Things got easier. I began learning how to live again. How to breathe again. How to find joy in the little things. There were still days I thought about him—actually, every day, if I'm honest. But with time, I learned how to hold those thoughts differently. How to smile when he crossed my mind, take a breath, and then keep moving.

We hadn't spoken in months. And I wasn't going to reach out. Why would I? I was just someone from his past. Maybe he loved me once. But that version of us no longer existed.

He had moved on. He was with someone. And I couldn't just show up in his life again, say *hi,* and pretend like I hadn't been replaced. That wouldn't be fair. I had to let him go. To free him—and myself—from the burden of me.

And yet, I don't know if I ever truly did. A part of me always stayed tethered to him, even when I told myself I had let go. It was as if some invisible thread still pulled at me, reminding me that no matter how much distance stretched between us, I was never completely free.

Then one day, I found out one of his closest friends had passed away. The news hit like a sudden storm, sharp and disorienting. She was too young, too vibrant, too full of light and laughter to be gone so soon. The kind of soul you imagine lasting forever. And just like that, she wasn't here anymore.

Something inside me broke when I heard it. Not only for her, but for him. For the emptiness I knew he must have felt, for the silence that follows grief when the world keeps moving but your heart doesn't.

I knew how much she meant to him. How intertwined their lives had been. And even from far away, even in the silence that separated us, I could feel the weight of his loss pressing against me.

It was as if his grief crossed the distance and found me. I carried a piece of it, quietly, invisibly, mourning not only her but the part of him that would never be the same again. And in that moment, my own heart cracked open—not for what we had lost between us, but for what he had lost forever.

All I wanted was to be with him. To hold him. To tell him, *You're not alone. I'm here. We'll get through this together.*

But I couldn't.

So I did the only thing I could do. I sent him a message. Simple, sincere, and from the bottom of my heart.

"Hey... I just heard about your friend. I'm so sorry. I know how much she meant to you. Please know I'm thinking of you—and despite everything, I'm still here if you ever need me."

I wasn't expecting a response. That message wasn't for me. It was for him. To know someone still cared. That I still cared.

There's a different kind of pain that comes when you lose someone young—someone just starting their life. The grief feels heavier. The shock deepens. The unfairness is louder.

The next day, my phone lit up with a message. It was him.

I froze. My heart started racing. I felt every emotion at once—hope, fear, gratitude, grief. But I didn't want this to be about me. I wanted to be strong. For him.

"Thank you. That... really means a lot."

His words were short, but warm. I read them once, then again, like maybe if I looked hard enough, I'd find more hidden between the lines. Gratitude. Relief. A softening I hadn't felt from him in so long. It meant something to him—I knew it did. And in that moment, the universe didn't just close a door—it cracked open a new one.

"I just want you to know I'm here. Thinking of you."

For a moment, there was silence. That awful silence where you start to doubt if you should have reached out at all. My chest tightened, my thumb hovered over the screen, tempted to unsend, to retreat. But then—

*"I'll be in New York soon. For the memorial. If you're open to it...
maybe we could meet. Talk."*

My heart leapt, my breath caught in my throat. A hundred
thoughts collided—what it would feel like to see him again, what I
would say, whether this was healing or danger. But the answer came
out of me before doubt could interfere.

"Yes. Of course, yes. Any time. Anywhere."

And as I hit send, my pulse raced. It wasn't just a message—it was
the beginning of something shifting.

A few days later, we made plans. It was one of those cold, crisp
winter days where the air stings your face but the sky is a flawless blue,
the kind of sun that tricks you into thinking it's warmer than it is. I
waited outside my apartment, my breath visible in the frozen air, my
hands tucked deep in my pockets to hide the nervous energy running
through me.

And then there he was. Walking toward me, bundled in his coat,
looking both exactly the same and somehow different. Seeing him
again after so long felt surreal—like stepping into a dream where everything is familiar, but not quite in the way you remember.

We decided to walk downtown to try a rice pudding place he had
mentioned. Something small and simple, but it felt like more. The
streets were alive with the sharp rhythm of winter—boots crunching
on salted sidewalks, the wind whipping through narrow alleys, people
rushing by in scarves and hats.

At first, it felt awkward, like two strangers catching up after years
apart. We talked about small things—work, travel, the weather. My
voice felt too careful, his smile a little guarded.

But after a few blocks, something shifted. The edges softened. The
laughter came easier, the pauses less heavy. The rhythm of walking side
by side pulled us into a flow, and before I knew it, we were sharing
little stories, trading jokes, letting the conversation find its own pace.

I was grateful. Grateful just to walk with him, to hear his voice in
real time instead of in memory, to exist in the same space without the
ache swallowing me whole.

We finally got to the pudding shop, half frozen but smiling, our
cheeks red from the wind. Stepping inside felt like slipping into another world—warm air wrapping around us, the sweet scent of sugar

and spice filling every corner. For a moment, it was enough just to thaw out, to sit across from him with the simple comfort of something sweet waiting to be chosen.

We debated flavors like it mattered more than it did, teasing each other over the choices. I went for chocolate—my forever weakness. (Well, second to him.) He chose vanilla with fruit—classic, clean, simple. Exactly him.

We sat down at a small table by the window, spoons in hand, the world outside still rushing by in the cold. For a while, we just talked. Nothing earth-shattering, nothing that would change our story. Little things, light things.

But beneath it, a current tugged at me. I wanted to ask so many things—questions that had lived in me for months. Why he pulled away. Why he chose someone else. If he ever thought of me, missed me, loved me still in some small, hidden way.

But I didn't ask. I couldn't. I didn't want to reopen the past, didn't want to risk bleeding again in front of him. I didn't want to relive the sharp edges of that pain. So instead, I let it go. I let the moment be what it was—simple, fragile, enough.

But there was one question I couldn't leave unasked. It had lived in me too long, gnawed at me in quiet moments, demanded its voice now that we were face-to-face again.

"Why didn't you tell me about your boyfriend that night?"

My voice was soft, careful, almost afraid of breaking the fragile peace between us.

He froze for a second, his eyes searching mine, as if weighing whether honesty would open another wound or finally close one.

"I didn't know how," he said at last, his voice low. *"I didn't want to hurt you. I knew it would break your heart."*

A lump rose in my throat. *"I would've understood,"* I whispered. *"Maybe not completely in that moment—maybe it would've crushed me. But at least I wouldn't have been left in the dark. It's the silence that hurt more. It's always the silence."*

He exhaled, his shoulders slumping a little. *"I didn't know what to say,"* he replied, almost like an admission, almost like an apology. His eyes softened, and for the first time, I believed him.

For a while, neither of us spoke. The noise of the shop carried around us—the clink of spoons, the hum of conversation, the shuffle of boots on the floor—but between us, there was only stillness.

And with that, without needing more words, we understood. We couldn't keep reopening old wounds, couldn't keep pulling each other back into the ruins of what had already burned down. The past was unchangeable, untouchable. But the present—the fragile, imperfect now—was still ours to shape.

And with that, we agreed to stop reopening old wounds. To stop trying to rewrite the past. Instead, we'd try—just maybe—to build something new. Something gentler. Something rooted in friendship, if that's where life wanted to take us.

Something different. Something better. Something honest.

When the last piece of us was gone, I thought I could rebuild myself from the emptiness. But emptiness isn't foundation—it's a void.

✦ ✦ ✦

"Letting go doesn't always mean forgetting. Sometimes it just means choosing to carry the memory without the weight."

Chapter 24

The Space I Tried to Fill

*"Sometimes the hardest place to stand is in the
space someone never fully made for you."*

After that meeting, I never truly knew where I stood with him anymore. There was one question that started knocking on the back of my mind, over and over, trying to fill in the blanks he left behind: Who was I to him?

We weren't boyfriends. We weren't lovers. We weren't even friends—not the way he had friends. But we weren't strangers either. So what were we? Where did I fit in his world?

There had to be a space, some category he placed me in. I needed to know—not because I needed more, but because I needed to know how to show up. How to exist without feeling like a burden. How to not push him away again.

He told me many times that we were friends. That he cared for me. That he saw me as part of his life, like he saw his other friends. And I wanted to believe that. I truly did. For a long time, I lived in that belief.

"We're friends," I told myself. *"We're part of each other's lives."* And I should be grateful, right? I could've lost him completely. But I didn't. He was still here. And so was I.

Still, something inside me didn't fully believe it. Because believing is one thing. But feeling it—truly feeling it—is another. It didn't feel like home. It felt hollow. It didn't feel right.

Because I had seen how he was with his actual friends. How he laughed with them. How relaxed he was. How fully present he showed up. I saw how they fit into his life so effortlessly. I watched the ease, the lightness, the belonging—and I realized I had never felt that.

I was there, but not really in it. Like I was standing just outside the circle, close enough to see the warmth but too far to feel it. I was something else. Something unspoken. Something undefined. Something even he wasn't sure what to do with.

He tried. I know he did. And I tried too. But neither of us could fully place me in his world. And over time, that began to break me.

All I ever wanted—just once—was to feel like a priority to him. To feel chosen. The way I always, always chose him. But no matter how hard I tried, no matter how much I gave or how patiently I waited, I always ended up feeling like an option.

He never invited me to group dinners, to parties, to birthdays. He never included me in his celebrations, the way he did with his other friends. He never reached for me in the ways I reached for him. He never posted a picture with me the way he did with his other friends…

And I never asked. I was too scared. Too scared he'd think I was too much. Too scared he'd walk away again.

He told me I mattered. He told me I was his friend. But his actions whispered something different.

He'd make plans and cancel. Reschedule. Shift things around because someone else came up. When we did spend time together, it was always just enough to keep me there. Just enough to keep the hope alive. But never more.

Maybe I was just greedy. Maybe I wanted too much. Maybe, deep down, I still loved him more than I admitted—and no amount of time would ever feel like enough.

So I told myself it was fine. That I was being sensitive. That he was busy. Spontaneous. Free-spirited. That I couldn't ask for more.

Because friendship isn't about expectations, right? Because real friendship should be unconditional.

Until I realized I was always the one who adjusted, the one who waited, the one who swallowed my needs just to be allowed to stay. Until I realized he never invited me to visit. Never asked to come see me. Never made space.

The only times I saw him… were the times I invited myself.

Once, before Christmas, I told him I was going to Miami and asked if I could stop by on the way to Orlando. The truth is—I wasn't going to Miami at all. I made that up. I just wanted to see him. I flew there for a single day, just to deliver his Christmas gift in person.

He offered his place, said he had to work, but would have time later. He dropped me off at a park while he worked.

Five hours passed. But I didn't mind.

Because after that, we had dinner. We saw a show. We shared a moment.

And the next morning, I left.

He never asked me to stay longer.

The second time was for his birthday. I asked if I could take him to dinner. He said yes.

"Come Sunday," he said. *"I'm off Monday. We can spend time together."*

I waited to book my flight.

When I finally asked, *"How early do you want to get rid of me?"*—half-joking, half-hoping he'd say, *"Stay a little longer"*—he said:

"I wish I could keep you longer, but I'm going on a cruise Monday morning with a coworker. I'll head to the airport at 10, you can fly out then."

And something inside me broke.

Not because of the cruise—I was happy he was going, I truly was. But because I only found out when I asked. Because he had so much time to tell me, and didn't. Because I realized—again—I wasn't a priority. I was a placeholder. A slot to fill. A convenience.

I wasn't enough for him to consider moving the cruise or not going; the cruise with a coworker was better than time with me.

And in that moment, I felt it fully:

I was never his priority. I was never his plan. I was never truly seen.

I was the stand-in. The easy option. The "yes" that waited patiently while everything else came first.

And that broke something in me.

But in a strange, painful way... it also freed me.

Because when you stop hoping, you stop hurting. When you stop expecting, you stop being disappointed. When you stop begging for a seat at someone else's table, you start building your own.

I wanted to be chosen. To be seen. To be loved, even platonically, with the same depth I gave.

But I had to face the truth: You cannot force someone to see your value if they're not looking. You cannot pour endlessly into someone who leaves you thirsty. You cannot keep proving your worth to someone who treats your presence as optional.

It's not love if it requires you to shrink. It's not friendship if it constantly leaves you starving.

That was the hardest lesson of all.

I had to stop begging for the bare minimum and start giving myself the love I was waiting for from him.

I had to learn that I am not a filler. I am not a placeholder. I am not the "just in case."

I am not too much. I was just never given enough.

And maybe the most powerful thing you can ever do... is walk away from the places where you're only ever tolerated, where you're just an option.

And choose yourself instead.

Even if it breaks your heart. Even if it's lonely. Even if it leaves a silence so loud it echoes for months.

Because real healing begins the moment you finally say:

"I deserve more than this."

And you walk away—not because you don't care anymore, but because you finally do. You care enough... to choose yourself.

Still, I stayed silent. I didn't speak up. I didn't ask for more.

Because I was terrified. Terrified that if I said how I really felt, he'd pull away completely. Even as just a friend.

So I swallowed it. I dimmed my light. I told myself scraps were enough, as long as I didn't lose him entirely.

I made myself small so he would let me stay.

I convinced myself that loving him meant sacrificing parts of myself.

And still, I believed he cared. In his own way. Deeply. Because even after everything—all the highs and lows—we were still trying. Not to be lovers. Not even to be best friends. But to be something. To stay in each other's lives.

And I know it wasn't easy for him either. I know he had his own fears. His own walls. His own way of loving that didn't always match mine. I don't believe he ever meant to hurt me—not intentionally. He just didn't always know how to hold me. To see me in the way I needed.

Whenever he came to New York, I wanted to see him. To spend time with him. To feel close again.

But he was distant. He came for his friends. He stayed with them. And when he did make time for me, it was always last-minute. Always at the very end.

And I got angry.

Not because I wanted more. But because I wanted to matter.

If he cared, wouldn't he want to see me the way I wanted to see him? Wouldn't he make time the way I always did?

That summer, he spent weeks in New York. Stayed with his friend. We saw each other a few times. It felt easier. More effortless. We weren't trying to be anything. Just friends.

We talked more. Shared more. Got closer.

He invited me to dinner the night before he was leaving. I was grateful. I was excited.

And then he canceled. Last-minute. No real explanation.

"We'll see each other next time," he said.

And something in me finally snapped.

I told him: *"You always do this. You always put me last. You always cancel on me. You always say 'next time.' It's fine. You don't need to apologize. I got the message."*

"People make time for who they want to make time for. Somehow, you always have time for your friends, for others. But not for me. I have always been just an option to you, and that hurts. Because to me, you've always been a priority."

"I tried so hard. I tried to earn your love. Your friendship. A place in your life. But the more I try, the more I feel pushed away. I don't deserve that. I ignored others for you. And you ignored me for them."

Once I started, I couldn't stop. I needed him to hear me.

But he didn't.

He responded: *"Mariusz, so many things happened this weekend at my friend's place. You have no idea. I won't apologize because I was where I needed to be. I love you. I was trying to be closer to you. But you can't judge what you don't know."*

I wasn't judging him. Never. All I wanted was honesty. Openness. A chance to understand.

But how could I understand something he never shared?

All I knew was what he allowed me to know.

And that was our last conversation. For a long time.

We didn't speak for over five months.

I wanted to reach out. To fix what I thought I broke. But I didn't know how.

I was scared. Scared to look needy again. Scared to show up first.

And I didn't want to make it seem like everything he did was okay. Because it wasn't. We both had failed. We both didn't communicate our feelings.

And the silence grew.

His 30th birthday came. A milestone. A day I had once imagined celebrating with him—surprises, laughter, maybe even a toast to the time we had shared. I had a gift ready, something I had picked out months earlier when hope still felt like enough to carry me. It sat on my dresser, wrapped neatly, waiting for hands that would never open it.

I had always been that way with him. Organized, thoughtful, planning ahead—birthdays, Christmas, little moments in between. It was my way of saying, *"You matter. I see you. I remember."* Every year since we met, he had received something from me. A token of care. A promise.

But this year felt different. He was thirty, and yet the only thing between us was silence. The gift sat untouched, and I told myself I wouldn't be the first to break it. This time, I wanted him to reach out. To say something. To remind me I wasn't the only one who still cared.

He didn't. And neither did I.

Still, I couldn't help myself. I wrote a message. I had it all typed out—*"Happy Birthday. I hope you know I'm thinking of you."* My thumb hovered over the send button, heart pounding, desperate to close the distance. But my hand froze. Fear, pride, the quiet ache of self-protection—they all tangled together until I couldn't move. So I didn't send it.

The next morning, the guilt hit me hard. The gift still sat there, mocking me. Every time I walked past it, my chest tightened. How could I not wish him a happy birthday? How could I ignore a day that meant so much? He meant everything to me, and yet my silence had become my only offering. I told myself I was protecting my heart, but deep down, it felt like I had failed him.

Then Christmas came. Another chance, another test. The city glowed with lights strung across streets, store windows filled with trees and ornaments, strangers humming carols under their breath. But between us—nothing. No call. No text. No attempt.

I stared at my phone on Christmas morning, half-hoping it would light up with his name. It didn't. I drafted another message, even pulled out the old gift, wondering if mailing it would say what I couldn't. But the weight of silence was stronger than any intention.

We were both waiting—for the other to blink first. Both too hurt, too proud, too scared. And so the days slipped by, each one heavier than the last. Milestones that should have been shared became markers of distance. The unopened gift gathered dust, but I couldn't bring myself to put it away. It stood as proof that, even in silence, I still thought of him. Always.

Rio.

Before we lost contact, he had mentioned—almost casually—that he might go for New Year's Eve. The words had stuck with me, lingering like an echo I couldn't quite let go of. And as it turned out, I was going too, with friends.

I didn't know what Rio would bring. The city itself felt like a dream—fireworks over the ocean, music in the streets, champagne flowing like water, strangers dancing barefoot in the sand. It was a place where anything could happen, where endings and beginnings blurred under the same sky.

But as much as I looked forward to it, a quiet part of me wasn't thinking of the parties or the lights. It was thinking of him.

I didn't even know if we'd see each other. Rio is vast, chaotic, alive with millions of people on New Year's Eve. But something in me held onto the smallest hope that life—just this once—might bend in my favor. That fate might step in and offer a moment of grace.

A chance to see him. A chance to know if there was still something left between us. Or if the silence, stretched so long and so heavy, had already spoken the truth for us both.

So I carried this fragile picture in my mind, tucked away like a secret: of running into him on the crowded streets of Rio. Of finding him in the very place where it had all begun. Of looking at him again not through memory, not through messages unsent, but in the flesh—real, undeniable, standing in front of me.

And maybe—just maybe—on that night of endings and beginnings, we could finally put the hurt and pride aside. Maybe we could see what was left when all the noise fell away.

Even if it was only for a moment.

✦ ✦ ✦

"Some stories don't end where the silence begins. Sometimes, the silence is just the pause before the heart decides to speak again."

Chapter 25

The Night I Stopped Chasing Love

*"You can't make someone choose you—but you
can choose to stop waiting. And in that choice,
you begin to come home to yourself."*

Rio de Janeiro.
What a beautiful place—alive with energy, rhythm, and light.
The warmth of the sun, the kindness of the people, the wild beauty
of nature, and the city woven into one seamless, vibrant heartbeat.
It felt like magic. And as the New Year approached, that magic only
grew.

I was there with my friends, surrounded by laughter and music,
the promise of fresh beginnings floating in the summer air. Everyone
was heading to Copacabana Beach, dressed in white, ready to welcome
the new year with open arms and hopeful hearts.

I smiled. I laughed. I danced. I tried. I truly tried.

But somewhere deep down, there was still a flicker of something
else… Hope.

Not just for the new year, but for something older. Something
unresolved. Some part of me was still holding on to the chance I might
run into F here, in this city, in this dreamscape. That maybe, just
maybe, fate would let us start over. Not from where we left off—but
from a gentler place. A clean slate.

There was a party that night, on top of Sugarloaf Mountain. It felt surreal—almost like a dream I didn't want to wake up from. The city glittered below us, Rio wrapped in lights like a necklace of fireflies. The music pulsed through the air, softening the distance between strangers. And standing tall in the distance was Christ the Redeemer, illuminated and still—arms wide open as if offering a silent blessing over the city.

I felt something sacred in the air. Maybe it was peace. Maybe forgiveness. Maybe just a temporary escape from all the questions I hadn't yet answered.

For a brief moment, I allowed myself to believe that I was exactly where I needed to be. That maybe, just maybe, life was beginning to soften.

I took a deep breath, letting the humid air fill my lungs. There was stillness in my chest—a kind of calm I hadn't felt in a long time. The noise of the world faded—the heartbreak, the questions, the longing. I felt weightless. Almost free.

And then I saw them—his friends.

Everything inside me stilled. My heart. My breath. The soft edges of peace I had just begun to taste... all of it paused.

And I knew.

I knew he was there.

I tried not to look for him. I told myself I wouldn't. I told myself I came here to feel free, to let go, to dance beneath the stars without chasing ghosts. But my eyes betrayed me. My heart betrayed me.

Even surrounded by music, laughter, and the breathtaking view of Rio's skyline—he was all I could feel. My gaze swept across the crowd like a reflex I couldn't shut off, searching for a face I hadn't seen in months...

A face I still saw every day in memory. In silence. In dreams I didn't ask for.

And then—there he was.

My breath caught in my chest. Everything around me faded, like a camera lens pulling focus until there was only him. But he wasn't alone.

He was with someone. Not his boyfriend. Someone new.

They were dancing. Laughing. He leaned in close. Their foreheads touched. Their hands slid together like it wasn't new—like it wasn't uncertain.

And then they kissed.

Not out of impulse. Not for attention. It was soft. It was real.

And it shattered something in me I thought had already turned to dust.

I stood frozen, trying to find the ground beneath my feet. I must've looked like I'd seen a ghost.

But the truth was—the ghost was me. The ghost of someone who still believed. Still loved. Still hoped.

And just like that... I was invisible again.

He saw me. I know he did.

For a second—just one second—our eyes met across the blur of bodies and flickering lights. The music didn't stop, but my world did.

And in that second, I wondered—could he feel it too?

We spoke. Briefly. Our words were clumsy, almost absurd against the beat of the night, the echo of the crowd, the laughter that felt so far from where I stood emotionally. It was like trying to whisper something sacred inside a thunderstorm.

This wasn't the moment I had imagined a hundred different ways. Not the gentle reunion. Not the quiet apology. Not the soft place to land where the ache could finally rest.

But still, I asked. I asked if we could meet. Really meet. Somewhere quieter. Somewhere honest.

Somewhere where the walls could drop and the truth could breathe.

He said yes.

The word landed in my chest like a fragile light. A promise. A thread. A beginning.

Or so I thought.

But then—just like that—he slipped away again. Not into the night. But into someone else's arms.

And I stood there, still holding the weight of that yes, while he let it go like it meant nothing.

I stood frozen, watching the way his body leaned toward theirs, the way his smile curved with ease, the way his hand found a home that wasn't mine.

And the distance between us was no longer measured in steps, but in the weight of a truth I could no longer ignore.

I was left standing in the middle of that celebration— the music shaking the walls, people pressing close all around me— and yet, I had never felt lonelier.

I waited that night. For the message. For the plan. For the effort that would prove his yes had meant something.

I waited the next night. And the next.

But nothing came. No message. No plan. No effort.

Only silence— a silence louder than the party, louder than the music, louder than any goodbye could have ever been.

And then New Year's Eve arrived. The night of beginnings. The night of hope. The night when the world holds its breath, waiting for the clock to strike twelve—for champagne, for confetti, for promises of change and love and second chances.

But not for me.

For me, it was a night of endings. A night of quiet collapse behind the noise.

Everyone else counted down with laughter and kisses, and I sat in the silence of a truth I could no longer run from.

That's when something in me shifted.

Not dramatically. Not with fireworks or grand gestures. But quietly. Painfully. Finally.

I realized—he didn't want to see me. If he had wanted to, he would have. If he had cared, he would have made space.

Because no one is ever too busy for the people they truly love.

And that realization, as sharp as glass against my chest, cut me open in the cleanest way possible. It hurt, yes. But it also set me free.

All this time, I had clung to the fragile idea that I still mattered to him. That somewhere in his thoughts, I was tucked away—a memory he turned to when the nights got quiet. That maybe I was still loved, just a little.

But I wasn't. And the silence had already been telling me so.

It wasn't easy to accept. It burned. It hollowed me out.

But beneath the ache was something steadier— a strange kind of peace.

Because when the truth finally lands, there's nothing left to chase.

No more maybes. No more ifs. Just the wide, open space of letting go.

And I stepped into that space, not unscarred, not unbroken— but lighter than I had been in months.

It wasn't easy. But it was okay.

I sent him a message that night—not out of desperation, not out of need—but because I wanted to release him. And maybe myself, too.

"I was really hoping we could talk before this year ends, to start the new year fresh—without weight, without silence between us. But I understand now that this conversation may not happen.

Still, I want you to know... I wish you nothing but happiness. Even if that happiness doesn't include me. Even if I'll never witness it again up close. You meant the world to me. You taught me what it feels like to love someone fully, without conditions. And even though it hurts deeply, I'm thankful—so thankful—that I got to feel that.

If I ever made you feel obligated to see me, I'm sorry. That was never my heart's intention. I just missed you—more than words could say. But I understand now. And I won't ask again.

Please know that no matter what, I'll always be in your corner. No expectations. Just love. I wish you a beautiful New Year. I hope it brings you everything your heart needs."

He replied. Kind. Brief. Distant.

"I didn't have time to meet you yesterday or today, but we still have a few days left. Thank you for the message. You know that I love you too and that you are an unconditional person in my life. I couldn't see you, sorry, it's been a wild weekend. I am going to NY this month, I'll try to catch up with you there. Have a safe flight..."

And just like that... another goodbye. This one colder. Softer. But final in a way the others hadn't been.

Final, I thought.

That night, beneath the fireworks of Rio, I learned one of the hardest truths of my life:

You can't force someone to care. You can't make someone show up. You can't convince someone to choose you—not with love, not with time, not with effort.

People make time for what matters. They find a way when they want to. They show up when it's real.

And if they don't—it's not about you. It never was.

It took me years to see that. To accept that the people we love most may not love us back the same way. That we can give everything and still not be chosen.

But that doesn't mean we're not worthy. It just means our love was meant for someone else.

So from now on, I will stop looking for people who are not looking for me. I will stop begging for a connection. I will stop shrinking to fit into the corners of someone else's life.

Because I deserve to be someone's priority. Someone's first choice. And one day, someone will choose me—with clarity, with joy, with open arms.

But until then… I choose myself.

And that is more than enough.

✦ ✦ ✦

"Sometimes the bravest thing you can do is stop chasing love—and let it find you when it's ready."

Chapter 26

Before Pride, There Was Pain

"Before Pride, there was pain. Before the rainbow, there was rain. Before celebration, there was silence."

Being gay isn't only about who you love—it's about surviving a world that once told you that your love should not exist.

It's growing up afraid of your own truth. It's hearing slurs before you even understand what they mean. It's watching how people shift around you when they sense something different—when your voice softens, when your laughter lingers, when your hands move too freely. It's realizing, far too young, that something about you unsettles others—even the ones who are supposed to love you the most.

So you start hiding. Silently. Skillfully. Every single day. You lower your voice. You guard your walk. You tighten your smile. You shrink your presence. Because the world teaches you to apologize for who you are long before you even know who that is.

Especially in small towns—especially in places like where I grew up in Poland—it's not just hard. It's suffocating. Where religion doesn't guide love but governs shame. Where tradition outweighs truth. Where silence feels safer than honesty. Where the Church carries more authority than empathy. And where being different doesn't just mean ridicule—it can mean danger.

I knew, even as a child, that the life I wanted—the life I needed—didn't exist there for someone like me. So I buried myself beneath layers of performance. I played along. I laughed when they laughed. I nodded when they nodded. I prayed when they prayed. I smiled. I went through the motions. But inside, I was aching. Gasping for breath. Dying to live.

And that's why, as soon as I could, I left. I didn't just leave Poland—I fled it. I ran to New York—not for the lights, not for the skyline, but for oxygen. For the right to exist. For the right to exhale without apology. I came here to live a real life, a whole life, one that didn't demand I cut myself into pieces just to be tolerated.

Because growing up where I did, I didn't just feel different—I felt wrong. Like a mistake. Like a sin. Like a secret my family prayed would never be spoken out loud.

And even now—even as an adult, even as someone who has come out—I still don't feel fully accepted. Not by them.

Everyone in my family knows I'm gay. It's not a secret. It hasn't been for a long time. But no one talks about it. It's as if there's an invisible wall built around that part of me. A quiet, unspoken agreement never to go near it. No questions. No curiosity. No conversations. Just silence—as though that part of me is too shameful, too uncomfortable, too foreign to acknowledge.

And I'd be lying if I said that didn't hurt.

Because sometimes, I want them to ask. I want someone to care enough to say, *"How are you, really?"* I want someone to ask, *"Are you in love?"* To wonder if there's someone special in my life. To ask, *"Do you feel seen? Do you feel safe? Do you feel loved?"*

But that question never came. And if I'm honest, I don't think it ever will.

They know who I am, but they don't know me. Because to know me, they'd have to face me. And to face me, they'd have to confront the truth they've spent a lifetime avoiding. They don't ask about my life because asking would mean accepting it. It would mean acknowledging the very parts of me they've chosen to keep in the dark.

So I've tried to be okay with that. Tried to build a life outside their silence. Tried to tell myself I don't need their validation, their questions, their words. But sometimes, I still ache for it. Not because

I need their approval— but because I want to be seen. I want to be known.

To my family: I love you. But I wish you loved all of me. I wish you asked. I wish you cared enough to ask. I don't want your tolerance. I don't want your silence. I want your voice. I want to know that you see me—not just the parts of me you can accept, but the whole of me. I want to know that your love isn't conditional on the pieces of myself I cut away to make you comfortable.

To the Church I grew up in: You taught me to kneel before God, but never taught me to stand in myself. You preached love but fed me shame. You told me God made me, then told me God didn't want me. You broke me in His name, and I will never forget that. But here's what I know now: If God is love, then He was never in your sermons. He was in the moments I survived despite them.

To the boy I used to be: I'm sorry you had to grow up in fear. I'm sorry you learned to hide before you learned to live. I'm sorry you believed you were a mistake. You weren't. You never were. And you never will be.

You were always worthy. You were always enough. You were always love in its purest form.

So many queer people live in this in-between space: Accepted, but not embraced. Known, but never really seen. Allowed in the room, but only if parts of us stay quiet at the door.

We carry that silence. We carry the weight of what was never said. The grief of a connection that never fully formed. We carry it through holidays, through birthdays, through every polite conversation that carefully avoids who we really are. And it hurts. Quietly, but constantly.

We talk about Pride—and we should. But before Pride, there was pain. Before the parades and the rainbows and the celebration, there were years of hiding. Years of shame. Years of pretending. Years of losing people we loved. Years of wondering if we would ever get to feel what others take for granted: belonging. Safety. Love.

Being gay should never have had to be a battle. But for so many of us, it has been. And for many, it still is.

We grow up believing we have to earn our place in this world. That we have to be better, smarter, more successful. That we must prove our worth ten times over just to be tolerated. That love—real love—is something reserved for other people, not for us.

But here's the truth: We were never the problem. We were never broken. We were never too much.

Being gay is not a failure to be straight. It is a truth. A flame. A kind of beauty the world has tried to erase but could never extinguish.

And if you're reading this—if you've ever felt like you were too much, too different, too unloved—please know this:

You are not alone. You belong. You always did. You don't have to prove your right to be here. You already do.

You are not the silence you grew up with. You are the voice you were born to use.

✦ ✦ ✦

"Before pride gave us wings, pain gave us roots. And those roots remind us: we are unshakable."

Chapter 27

When the Mind Breaks and the Body Follows

"There is a light that stays lit, even in the darkest nights—it lives in the quiet decision to keep breathing."

Lonely. Lost. Sad. Heartbroken. Hopeless. Defeated. These are the words I can name. But there are more—so many more—that live unnamed inside me. Emotions I don't know how to hold, pain I don't know how to release. Some days, I survive. Others, I drown.

There are days I feel completely alone. Not the kind of alone that comes from being by yourself—but the kind that fills a room even when it's crowded. Tears rise but won't fall. I ache to cry, to unravel, to let it all pour out. But I can't. And I don't know why. I'm full of feeling and yet numb. I'm overflowing and yet empty. How do you explain that?

I feel stuck—frozen in the middle of a life I can't seem to move forward in. I keep looking for signs, for someone to tell me where to go from here. But no one's coming with a map. No one's coming with answers. This is my journey. My confusion. My path to figure out. And that terrifies me.

I've started over so many times. I've let go of homes, jobs, dreams, people. I've tried. God, I've tried. And still—I feel like I'm standing still while everyone else keeps moving.

Everything around me feels like it's crumbling—my relationships, my future, my health. I don't even know where to begin picking up the pieces.

Right now, I don't have a home of my own. I'm staying with my cousins, and I'm grateful—I truly am. But inside, I feel homeless. Not just without a place, but without a sense of belonging. I walk through days like a ghost, trying to find a corner in someone else's world to feel safe in.

I keep telling myself it's temporary. That this moment will pass. That light will come. But when you live in darkness long enough, even hope starts to feel like a lie.

And then—my body broke.

I've never been good at putting myself first. I ignored my health. Skipped appointments. Dismissed symptoms. I thought I was just exhausted. I told myself it would pass. A nap, a meal, a weekend of rest. But it didn't.

Even after I tried to *do everything right*—eat well, move more, sleep enough—I was still drowning in fatigue. Still aching. Still dragging my body through days that felt too heavy to carry.

I told myself it was depression. Again. The same beast that's haunted me for years.

I know its voice. I know how it hides and waits. It doesn't knock—it slips in. It whispers: *You're a burden. You don't matter. You'll never feel better.*

And I listened.

There were nights I stood at the edge—not of a building, but of my will to stay. Nights when silence seemed kinder than survival. Nights when I imagined what it would be like to stop existing. To rest. To disappear.

But even then—a voice inside me whispered back: *Not yet. Please. Stay.*

I didn't choose depression, but I chose to live. Even when I didn't know how. Even when I didn't want to.

I looked for light. Even the tiniest flicker. A memory. A song. A kind word. I let those small things tether me to this world. And sometimes, that's enough.

I still want love. The kind that feels like home—not a battlefield. I want softness. I want something that doesn't break me to hold on to.

Mentally, I've learned how to fight. I've learned to talk back to the thoughts that want me gone. I've learned to breathe when my brain tells me not to. But my body... it hadn't caught up.

Even after all the right habits, the fatigue stayed. My body felt like it was screaming for help—but no one could hear it. Not even me.

I didn't have insurance. In this country, that means you don't exist. The system doesn't see your suffering—it sees a price tag. I was paying thousands for tests with no answers.

Until one day—someone finally looked closer. A doctor tested my thyroid.

Hypothyroidism. My body wasn't producing enough hormones. The fatigue, the weight, the sadness—it all started to make sense.

But then—another clue. A red patch on my chest. *Just sunburn,* I thought. *Just nothing.*

It wasn't.

More tests. More waiting. And then the words that shattered everything: *You have a type of blood cancer.*

Polycythemia vera. My bone marrow was producing too many red blood cells. My blood had become thick—dangerously so. Clots. Strokes. Heart attacks. It's not curable. But it's manageable.

Manageable.

What a strange word to hear when your world is falling apart.

Treatment began. Blood thinners. Blood draws. Monitoring. Fear. Hope. More fear.

Some days, I can walk. Others, I can't stand. My legs burn like fire. My body feels foreign—like it's betraying me with every breath.

I never asked for this. No one does. But here I am, surviving a life I never prepared for.

All I want is peace. Just one stretch of road that doesn't twist or break beneath me.

So now, I care for myself the way I've always cared for others. Gently. Patiently. Tenderly. I listen to my body now, because it's been screaming for years and I never heard it.

And in that silence—this truth rose: health is everything.

We don't see it until it's gone. Until the smallest things—getting out of bed, taking a breath, feeling safe in your skin—feel impossible.

Nothing else matters when you're not well. Not money. Not love. Not dreams. Because without your health, none of those things can be truly lived.

Now, I cherish the good days. I don't rush them. I don't overlook them. I treat energy as a gift, not a guarantee.

Because this body—this tired, aching, beautiful body—is the only home I have. And I want to stay.

And here's what I need to say louder than anything else: we need to talk about mental health.

Really talk. Not in hashtags. Not in passing. Not in shame.

We need to talk about the nights we don't post about. The ones where we curl up and wonder if we matter. The mornings when getting out of bed feels like climbing a mountain with broken legs.

We need to stop calling it weakness. Stop whispering about it like it's contagious. Stop pretending we're fine when we're falling apart.

Depression is not failure. Anxiety is not attention-seeking. Having suicidal thoughts doesn't make you broken—it makes you human in pain.

And I've been there. I've lived inside that darkness. I've begged the universe to take the pain away. I've wondered if anyone would notice if I disappeared.

But I stayed.

Not because I was brave. But because something inside me—a whisper, a breath, a heartbeat—refused to give up.

If you're there too—if you're in that quiet war with your own mind—I want you to hear this: you are not alone. Your pain is valid. Your life matters. There is help. There is hope. Even if you can't feel it yet.

Please—stay.

Ask for help. Speak your truth. Cry. Yell. Break down. Heal.

We need to create a world where it's safe to say, *"I'm not okay,"* and be met with compassion—not silence.

I've lived through the dark. I still visit it sometimes. But now, I know—there is light. Always. Somewhere.

You just have to keep breathing until you see it.

So don't give up. Not now. Not yet.

Let's stop pretending. Let's start healing. Let's keep each other alive.

I stayed. And I'm so, so glad I did. I hope you will too.

✦ ✦ ✦

"There is a light that stays lit, even in the darkest nights—
it lives in the quiet decision to keep breathing."

Chapter 28

The Love That Stayed

"Not every love story ends when the romance does. Some transform, soften, and stay—quiet, but eternal."

When everything else fell apart, a different kind of love showed up—the kind that didn't ask me to earn it. The kind that stayed.

You'd think after all the heartbreak, all the silence, all the times we said goodbye—our story would be over. But somehow, it wasn't. Not completely. Not yet.

Our love story, the romantic one, may have ended. But we—me and F—we weren't done. There was something still breathing between us. Something softer now. Quieter. But alive. And for the first time, it wasn't about holding on too tight, or trying to rewrite the past. It was about presence. About peace. About being in each other's lives without expectation, without pain, without pulling each other in and out of heartbreak. This wasn't the kind of love that asks for anything in return. This was love that simply... stayed.

After Rio—after that final goodbye that felt so final—I thought that was it. He had already moved on. Twice. It felt like he'd closed the door for good. But then weeks later, that door creaked open again. He came to New York. And he reached out.

This time—it was him. He was the one who wanted to see me. He was the one who initiated. And that small, simple gesture meant everything. It was a shift I never expected, a warmth I had stopped hoping for.

Maybe my last message in Rio meant something. Maybe he heard what I was trying to say—really heard it. Maybe, for the first time, he didn't feel pushed or guilted or trapped. Maybe he just felt loved. I didn't want to drown in maybes again, so I didn't overthink it. I simply said yes. Of course I wanted to see him. I always wanted to see him—even when it hurt. Especially when it hurt. Because seeing him meant I wasn't alone in the love.

We met at a restaurant. Neutral ground.

No pressure. No expectations. Just a table between us and the kind of silence that only exists when something unspoken has lived too long in the air.

And this time… we really talked.

Not the surface-level, easy-kind-of-conversation we used to slip into when things felt too fragile. Not the updates and polite check-ins. Not the laugh-and-deflect rhythm we had once mastered to avoid saying what truly needed to be said.

No—this was different.

There was a softness in the space between us. A mutual exhaustion from carrying too much for too long. And maybe… a shared readiness to finally set it down.

We spoke honestly. Gently. Loudly, in the way that feelings can be loud even when voices are low. It wasn't about volume—it was about presence.

Every word we shared felt weighted. Deliberate. Sacred. Not rehearsed, not filtered—just real.

We said the things we had buried beneath months of silence. We let the hurt show. We let the tenderness return. We didn't try to fix anything. We didn't pretend. We just… let the truth be seen.

And somehow, even in the middle of a crowded restaurant—with clinking glasses, background music, and the hum of other people's lives—it felt like the world had made space for this moment.

There were no dramatic declarations. No promises. Just two people, finally looking each other in the eye—without fear, without armor, without the need to win or be right.

Just two people who had once loved deeply, trying to understand what remained in the ashes. Trying to honor the connection, even if the shape of it had changed.

For the first time in a long time, it felt like neither of us was pretending. Not to each other. Not to ourselves.

And that honesty— It didn't solve everything. But it softened something. It stitched up a few old tears. It reminded us of the good beneath the wreckage.

And for a moment, it was enough.

And for the first time, I saw him. Not the version of him I had built in my head—the one who hurt me, avoided me, left me behind. I saw the real him. I saw how hard he had tried. How hard he is still trying.

He had been showing up in the only ways he knew how. Maybe not in the way I wanted. Maybe not with the timing I craved. But he was trying. He always had been.

I just couldn't see it before.

I was too consumed by my own pain, too lost in my own disappointment, to notice the ways he was holding on. I wanted him to show up perfectly. To say the right words, at the right time, in the right way. But love isn't perfect. And neither are we.

And now—I finally see him. I see his effort. I see his discomfort and courage and confusion and care, all tangled up together. And I see myself, too. The version of me that couldn't see beyond my own hurt. The version that centered my own story so tightly that I forgot he had one too.

I carry that regret. Because if I had seen him clearly then… maybe we could've saved ourselves a lot of pain. But I didn't. I see him now.

And he sees me, too.

Since that day, something shifted between us. We began texting more. Talking more. But differently this time—lighter, freer, safer. We weren't afraid of saying too much or not enough. We weren't measuring our worth by how often we showed up. We just… did. Because we wanted to.

That feeling—that freedom—filled something in me I thought was permanently empty.

For the first time in so long, I felt like I was enough. Maybe not in the way I once hoped. But still... enough.

There's still a quiet hope inside me. A small, stubborn flicker that maybe one day, he'll see me the way he once did. But that hope is mine to hold quietly. I don't expect it to change anything. I've simply learned to live with it—not let it lead me.

Because the friendship we've built now is real. It's rooted in truth and acceptance, not fantasy and fear. And that's what matters most.

We've learned to be vulnerable with each other. To trust again. To be present—not perfect. We stayed. We chose to stay.

And I now see that he was always trying. In his way. In the best way he could. I just didn't have the eyes to see it then.

I see it now.

And I see myself, too.

It's taken me a long time to understand that before we can ever truly see someone else—we have to be willing to see ourselves. To accept who we are. To forgive what we weren't ready for. To love ourselves deeply, so we can love others gently.

Because love without self-awareness becomes need. Love without self-acceptance becomes pain. Love without boundaries becomes obsession.

But real love—unconditional love—begins with knowing who you are. Not just what you want. And once you can offer that to yourself, you can finally offer it to someone else—without expectation, without fear, without demand.

I didn't know myself back then. He didn't either. We were both learning. But now... I know. I know who I am. I know what I need. And I know how to love without losing myself.

That's the love that stayed. The love we built after everything broke. The love we choose now, again and again. And this time... It's enough.

I am grateful for F. I always have been. But now—more than ever—I feel it in a deeper, quieter way. Not just for the love we once shared, or the memories we built through the chaos and uncertainty. But for him. For his presence in my life. For his soul, exactly as it is.

We went through so much—so many unknowns, so much unspoken pain, so many moments we didn't know how to navigate. But still, somehow, we found our way to something real. Imperfect. Messy. Human. But real.

And today, even after everything, we're still trying. Trying to be present for each other in the ways we can. Trying to understand. Trying to forgive. Trying to love—not just in the way the world defines it, but in a way that feels safe and true to us. And that effort... that quiet, sacred effort... means everything to me.

We are not perfect. We never were. We still hurt. We still misunderstand. We still fall short. But this time, we see each other more clearly. Not as fantasies, not as projections— But as we are.

And I choose him. Not an ideal version. Him.

I don't know what the future holds. I don't know where our paths will lead. But I do know this: He will always have a place in my heart that no one else will ever touch. And no matter what happens—whether we grow closer or drift apart—he will always have my love.

Without condition. Without expectation. Without pressure. Just love.

The kind that stays quietly in the background if it must, But never disappears. The kind that says, "I'm here. Always. In whatever way you need me to be."

And if one day our lives no longer intertwine, if silence takes the place of words, He can still reach out—and I'll be there. Because some connections are just... eternal.

And he is mine. Always, In the softest, most unshakable corners of my soul.

✦ ✦ ✦

"Some loves don't fade; they change form. They become quieter, deeper, and in that quietness—they endure."

Chapter 29

Learning to Understand Myself... and Him

"We spend years trying to understand others, but true healing begins the moment we dare to understand ourselves."

It took me a long time to understand myself—my feelings, my reactions, the fears I carried quietly but lived through loudly. And it took even longer to understand him. To understand us.

But maybe we're never meant to understand everything. People evolve. Emotions shift. Clarity arrives in waves—sometimes only after the storm has already passed. Still, if we can understand just enough—enough to stop blaming ourselves for every heartbreak, enough to extend compassion to our confused younger selves, enough to stop turning pain into proof that we're unlovable—then maybe that's where healing truly begins.

Because sometimes the fault isn't ours. Sometimes, we were simply doing the best we could with the tools we were handed—tools that were broken, missing, or heavy with old wounds.

We learn early. We learn to shut down or cling too tight. We learn to please, to perform, to shrink, to shout. We build walls or chase ghosts. But these aren't flaws. They are survival tactics. Echoes from the past.

We weren't born guarded. We weren't born needy, distant, or afraid of love. We became that way to protect ourselves.

The Patterns We Didn't Choose

Some of us learned that love meant proving ourselves—that being too much, too emotional, too needy would push people away. So we became anxious—constantly reaching, always scanning for signs of distance, ready to fight to keep love from slipping through our hands.

Others learned that closeness brought chaos—that intimacy came with demands, criticism, or pain. So we became avoidant—keeping people at arm's length, needing space to breathe, withdrawing the moment things got too close.

And when anxious meets avoidant, both fears ignite.

The anxious one reaches out: *"Please don't leave."* The avoidant one pulls back: *"Please don't come too close."*

And both end up hurting. Not because they don't care, but because their fears are dancing with each other instead of their hearts.

I was the anxious one. He was avoidant.

And for so long, I couldn't understand why every time I reached for him, he slipped further away. Why my need for reassurance triggered his need for space. Why I felt abandoned—and he felt smothered.

I needed closeness. He needed distance. I chased. He withdrew. I felt unloved. He felt overwhelmed.

We weren't failing each other. We were protecting ourselves the only way we knew how.

Two Glasses of Water

Think of it like this: we were two glasses of water—one tall, one short.

I was the tall glass, overflowing with love to give. I kept pouring and pouring into him, thinking more love would finally fill the emptiness between us. But his glass was smaller. He filled up quickly. He became overwhelmed, unsure of what to do with all that love—so he backed away.

He, in turn, poured everything he had into me. But because my glass was taller, it never felt like enough. I kept craving more, not realizing he was already giving all he could.

We weren't mismatched in how much we loved. We were mismatched in how we expressed love—and in what we needed to feel safe.

And for a long time, I couldn't see that. I only felt rejected.

But now... I understand.

He wasn't failing me. He was protecting himself. And I wasn't too much. I was simply asking for the kind of love I never got as a child.

We were both doing our best. Just with different blueprints.

The Healing That Comes With Understanding

I've learned that understanding your attachment style doesn't just heal your relationships—it heals *you.*

It gives you the language for your pain. The map to escape old cycles. The freedom to stop calling yourself "too much" or "not enough."

It shows you that you're human. Shaped by experience. But capable of growth.

I now see him more clearly. And I see myself more gently.

I don't regret loving him. I regret not seeing both of our wounds sooner. But I forgive myself. I was still learning. We both were.

Now, I know what I need. I know what I won't chase. I know what I deserve—and what I'm responsible for healing on my own.

And I've learned this: The greatest act of love is not to change someone. It's to *see* them.

The Truth That Changed Me

If there's one truth that changed me, it's this:

You cannot love someone else deeply if you do not first understand yourself. You cannot receive healthy love if part of you still believes you have to earn it. You cannot ask someone to make you feel secure if you haven't yet made peace with your past.

Self-awareness is not a luxury. It's a lifeline.

Because without it, we mistake distance for rejection instead of fear. We see silence as disinterest instead of protection. We call people cold when they're really just scared to be seen.

But once we understand ourselves—truly, gently, honestly—we begin showing up differently. We stop chasing. We stop withdrawing. We stop begging for love and start creating it—with presence, with boundaries, with patience.

Because real love—the kind that doesn't drown you or leave you thirsty—isn't about fixing anyone. It's about accepting them.

And the first person you must learn to accept... Is you.

"You can't truly love someone else until you understand the parts of you that once begged for love. Healing begins not in being chosen—but in choosing yourself."

Chapter 30

The Love That Asked for Nothing

"Unconditional love isn't about what you get—it's about what you give, even when it breaks you."

Iused to believe that if you fought hard enough for someone, they'd stay. That if you loved them with every inch of your soul, if you gave without holding back, if you showed up through the pain and silence and uncertainty—then surely... they'd stay. Surely, they'd choose you back.

But love doesn't work like that. Not always.

Sometimes, you can give your whole heart to someone... and they still walk away with it.

I fought. For every person I loved—I fought.

I bled in silence. I begged without words. I loved with a fire that burned through every wall they put up. I stayed long after I should've let go. I held on even when the silence screamed louder than their voice ever did. I held on even when I knew I was the only one left holding on.

And in the end, I still lost them. Every single one.

Not because I wasn't enough. But because I was always the only one trying.

For a long time, I thought I was the problem. Maybe I loved too much. Maybe I stayed too long. Maybe I should've been colder, harder, quieter.

But now I know the truth: There is no shame in loving deeply. There is no shame in giving fully. The shame belongs to those who couldn't show up for love that asked for nothing but honesty and effort.

I would've done anything to feel someone fight for me—for once. Not with flowers or promises or perfectly timed texts. Just… effort. Presence. Truth.

A hand that doesn't let go. A voice that says, *"You matter. I'm not leaving."*

But that moment never came.

Because most people choose the easy way out. Even when they care, they still run. Because staying requires work.

Love—real, lasting, soul-deep love—takes effort, accountability, and the courage to stay when everything in you wants to run.

But me? I'm not built to run.

When I love, I stay. I fight. I give until there's nothing left to give. I love even when I'm hurting. Even when I know I might be breaking alone.

And maybe that's why I've been shattered so many times. Because I kept handing my heart to people who didn't know how to hold it. Because I kept hoping that if I loved hard enough, they'd learn how to love me back.

But still—I have no regrets. Because I tried. I gave. I stayed.

And if my everything wasn't enough for them, that says everything about them—and nothing about me.

I will never apologize for how I love. And I will never stop believing in it.

Because love has carried me through hell. Through heartbreaks that made it hard to breathe. Through nights when I wanted to disappear. Through grief that gutted me from the inside out.

But love—my capacity to love—kept me going. Even when everything else failed. When I was drowning in my own sadness, love whispered, *"Keep going."*

And I did.

I still believe in a love that stays. A love that chooses you again and again, not just when it's easy—but especially when it's hard. A love that doesn't disappear when you're difficult or broken or scared. A love that says, *"We're in this together."*

One day, I will find that kind of love. And one day, I hope it finds me too.

A love that doesn't flinch at the weight of my heart. That doesn't require convincing or performing or shrinking. Someone who chooses me the way I always chose F.

And when that day comes, there will be no more begging. No more proving. No more wondering if I'm enough.

Because I will be. I always was.

And if that day never comes… If I never get that second love story with the happy ending… If the love I gave never makes its way back to me… I'll still be okay.

Because I know what it means to love with nothing held back. To give when there's nothing left. To forgive when it hurts. To choose someone even when they stop choosing you. To wish someone happiness while you're breaking.

That kind of love—it breaks you. But it also builds you. It leaves a mark. It becomes part of your story.

Even if it ends, even if it never comes back, unconditional love stays. It leaves behind something holy. Something real. A light. A truth. A reminder that you felt deeply in a world that keeps trying to make us feel less.

And that love—the love I gave, the love I never got to feel in return—that's the love that stayed with me.

One day, I hope to find the kind of love I don't just touch—but drown in. A love that wraps around me so fully that I can feel it in my breath, my skin, my bones.

Because I've already given that love. I've already lived it.

With F, I was only allowed to dip my toes in. At best, I got in up to my knees. Never deeper. Never all the way.

But even that—just that little taste—was enough to make me fight like hell. To stay. To hope. To believe that maybe, if I loved hard enough, it could be saved.

But that day never came.

And now, I carry a hope—not for someone perfect, but for someone brave enough to hold what I've always had to carry alone. For someone who will see the love I gave and finally say, *"Me too."*

✦ ✦ ✦

"Real love doesn't leave. And if it did, it was never real.
But the love you gave? That's real. And it still lives in you."

Chapter 31

When They Leave – Fractured Friendships and Those Who Stayed

"People come into our lives for a reason, a season, or a lifetime. The hardest part is learning which is which."

Some people enter briefly but leave behind echoes that never fade. Some walk beside us for a chapter, holding our hands through a moment in time. And a rare few—if we're lucky—stay. Through the mess. Through the healing. Through it all.

I used to believe—maybe I still do—that everyone who entered my life was meant to be forever. I didn't want temporary. I wanted soul ties, not passing phases.

Because the truth is, I don't connect easily. Not because I don't want to—quite the opposite. I connect too fast, too deep, too soon. I give all of me. I dive in with my whole heart. And I've learned that not everyone can meet me there. Some people can't meet you in the deep. Some people are scared of it. And some just... don't want to.

Trust is fragile. When it's broken, it's not easy to put back together. It takes time, effort, vulnerability—and not everyone is willing to do that work. Some people leave when the first cracks appear. They walk away when things get hard, not because they're bad people, but maybe because the fight isn't worth it to them.

Because relationships take two. Friendships take effort from both sides. And the harsh reality is—some people don't want to fight for you the way you're fighting for them. They let go when you're still holding on. They stop showing up right when you need them most.

But to me, it always has been. When I choose you—whether as a friend, a partner, a person—I stay. I fight. I show up. Even when I'm falling apart. Even when it's hard. That's just who I am.

But sometimes... that's not enough. Because connection is a two-way street. And not everyone chooses to walk it with you. Some people let go when you're still holding on. Some disappear when all you want is for them to stay.

I've felt that. Over and over. Especially in my darkest seasons—when life hit me hardest, when I was sick, heartbroken, tired of pretending I was okay—I watched people I loved simply vanish. People I would've done anything for. People, I did everything for. And when I stopped reaching out, my phone stopped ringing. The silence was brutal.

And yet... some people stayed.

They showed up for me at my worst, when I had nothing left to give. They didn't expect perfection or performance—they simply stayed. They held space for me. They were anchors when everything else felt like it was drifting away.

To Keith and Aric—my anchors, my brothers, my mirrors: thank you. You stayed. Through the storms. Through my silence. Through the days when I didn't have the strength to answer, to show up, or even say I was hurting. I know I wasn't always the best friend in those moments. When I disappear, it's not because I don't care—it's because I'm drowning. I isolate when I'm in pain. That's how I reset. That's how I survive. But you never took it personally. You never made me feel guilty for coping the only way I knew how. You waited. You checked in. You reminded me—gently, patiently—that I wasn't alone. You never gave up on me. Not even when I gave up on myself. You didn't just love the best version of me. You loved the broken one too. The silent one. The one that hid away and didn't always say thank you. You never expected me to perform. You just loved me as I was.

And more than that—you held up mirrors. You told me the truth. Even when it hurt. Especially when it hurt. You didn't sugarcoat the hard things. You called me out when I needed to wake up. You reminded me who I was when I forgot. You saw through me, even when

I tried to hide. You laughed with me, cried with me, yelled at me, and loved me—all at once. You were the friends who held my heart and my truth, even when I was too scared to face either. Friends like you are rare, and I am thankful for you every day.

If anyone out there has friends like that—please, protect them. Fight for them. Love them loudly. Because people like that don't come around often.

To Marie, my pink dragon—you were a spark of magic in my life.

To Vitor, my family, my soul friend—you've stood by me through storms.

To Ewelina, my very first friend in New York—you've always been there. Always. You never gave up on me.

To Daniel, my oldest, wildest, truest—you knew me when I didn't know myself. I miss you every day and can't wait until we live in the same city again.

To Tyler and Damir, whom I met on sacred soil in Peru—our souls recognized each other instantly. Thank you for seeing me.

To Agnieszka, my cousin but really my sister—you've been my rock, my heart, my shelter. I love you more than I can put into words.

To Sara and Alejandro, my dearest Spanish teachers and even dearer friends—you understand me in ways few people ever have. Thank you for staying. Thank you for loving me in all the quiet ways.

To Jamie, our friendship has had its ups and downs, but deep down, we sincerely care for each other.

To all of you—thank you. Thank you for not leaving. Thank you for choosing me when I had nothing to give. Thank you for standing by me when I didn't even recognize myself. Thank you for being proof that real friendship still exists. You were my light in the darkest hours. You are my people. And I hope you know—I'm yours. Always.

And yet, I still grieve the friendships that faded. The ones that fractured. Especially the ones that ended without closure—just silence and distance. I still care. I still love. But I don't know how to fix what broke. I wish I did.

There's one friendship in particular that still hurts—one that changed overnight. We were so close for years. Then one weekend— one wild, messy, imperfect weekend—it all shattered.

It was Memorial Day, Fire Island. Our annual escape, our little tradition. That year, I was carrying more than usual—pain, stress, emotional exhaustion. I wanted to forget. I wanted to feel free. I wanted to be okay, even for just a few days.

There were drinks, there were drugs. I let go. Maybe I was too much. Maybe I said things I shouldn't have. But I thought they knew me—I thought he knew me. I thought the people who loved me understood that when I tease, when I'm loud, when I'm playful—it's often how I show love.

But after that weekend, I got a message. Cold. Sharp. Accusing me of being mean, of having a drug problem, of heading for rehab, or worse. Ten years of friendship… gone with one judgmental text.

What hurt the most wasn't the accusation—it was how quickly he chose to see the worst in me. How quickly he forgot everything we'd shared. I never judged him when he stumbled. I always saw him, the real him—beyond the moments. But he couldn't do the same for me. He gave up on me.

And I still miss him. I miss the connection. The laughter. The friendship. I still care deeply. But I'm scared. I'm scared that trying to fix it might reopen wounds. I'm scared of getting hurt again.

We still see each other, sometimes—surrounded by mutual friends. We're polite. Distant. Strangers with a shared past. It breaks my heart. Because I didn't see it coming. I still don't fully understand how it ended so fast. Maybe one day we'll talk. Maybe we'll own our pain, our pride, and our parts in it. Or maybe… that was our season. And it's over.

Friendship is raw. It's messy. It's beautifully imperfect. It's not supposed to be effortless. It's supposed to be real. Sometimes, no matter how much you love someone, they leave. Sometimes, they walk away when you need them most. And that's one of the hardest truths to live with.

But maybe… endings aren't always failures. Maybe the purpose of some friendships isn't to last, but to teach. To remind you of what you deserve. To show you what love is—and what it's not.

Some people come into your life to hold your hand through the dark. Some to teach you how to let go. And a rare few… stay. No matter what.

Fight for those people. Say the hard things. Say the true things. Apologize when it matters. Show up. Stay. And if someone stays for you—hold them close. Because in this world, love without condition is a treasure.

To the ones who left: I forgive you. To the ones who stayed: I love you. And to those I've yet to meet—may we be brave enough to try again.

✦ ✦ ✦

"Real friendship doesn't ask you to be perfect. It just asks you to stay."

Chapter 32

The Hardest Truth Is the One We Already Know

"Sometimes, the truth doesn't shatter us—it frees us. But only after it breaks everything we were never meant to hold on to."

There are some truths we spend our whole lives running from. Some words we pray we'll never hear. Some realizations we bury under distractions, under hope, under noise—because to face them would mean facing the very pain we're not ready to feel. So we delay it. We pretend. We wait. We convince ourselves that if we just hold on a little longer, things will get better. That maybe they'll change. That maybe we won't have to let go.

But the truth doesn't disappear just because we look away. It waits. Patiently. Quietly. And then one day, when we're too tired to run, too broken to fake it—it hits. Hard.

Like a bullet to the soul. And suddenly, everything we tried not to feel comes flooding in all at once.

I've been there. I've swallowed the lump in my throat to keep the peace. I've smiled when I wanted to scream. I've avoided the hard conversations. Bit my tongue when I should've spoken. Stayed when I should've walked away. Smiled when I was silently breaking.

And every time I ignored the truth, it didn't vanish—it just grew heavier. Until it crushed me.

And that's the thing: The hardest truth is usually the one we already know.

Deep down, we always know. We know when someone doesn't love us the way we need to be loved. We know when we're being taken for granted. We know when the effort is one-sided.

But we lie to ourselves with hope. We say, *"Maybe they just need more time." "Maybe I need to try harder." "Maybe if I just hold on a little longer..."*

But *maybe* is how we bleed out quietly.

We try. We give. We bend ourselves in half hoping someone will finally notice us, appreciate us, choose us the way we keep choosing them. We pour every last ounce of ourselves into the relationship, the job, the friendship—until there's nothing left but the echo of our own unmet needs.

And when they still don't choose us, it feels like we've failed. Like we weren't enough. Like maybe love really is something you have to earn.

But here's the real truth—the one I had to learn the hard way: You can give everything to the wrong person, and it still won't be enough.

Not because you aren't enough. But because they weren't ready. Or they didn't care. Or they didn't know how to love beyond their own wounds and limitations.

And that's not your fault. It's not your job to fix someone else's emotional unavailability. It's not your role to make them whole. And you are not required to stay in spaces where you are shrinking just to fit.

We need to stop trying to earn love.

Real love doesn't make you feel invisible. It doesn't make you question your worth. It doesn't keep you waiting in emotional purgatory.

Love is not something to chase. It's something that's freely given by the right people—the ones who see your worth even when you're not at your best.

I know it's hard to let go. To walk away from something you poured your entire soul into. To release a dream, a connection, a version of yourself you've built your life around.

But holding on to what's hurting you isn't loyalty—it's fear. Fear of starting over. Fear of being alone. Fear that maybe this is all we'll ever get.

But here's the truth beneath the fear: Sometimes, the bravest thing you can do is choose yourself.

Not out of bitterness—but out of self-respect. Because when you keep choosing people who don't choose you, you slowly start to forget how to choose yourself.

You lose yourself in the process of trying to matter to someone who was never capable of truly seeing you. You forget your own worth while desperately trying to prove it. You abandon yourself trying to hold together something that was never solid to begin with.

And that's not love. That's self-erasure.

You matter. You are enough. You deserve to be loved loudly and clearly. Without begging. Without shrinking. Without breaking.

No one—no partner, no boss, no friend, no family member—has the right to treat you like you're disposable. I don't care how much power they have, how much money they make, how charming or successful they seem.

Nothing gives someone the right to make you feel like you are small.

Because you are not small. You are not invisible. You are not less than.

And if someone makes you question that—if they chip away at your self-worth—walk away.

It's not your job to convince someone of your value. It's your responsibility to protect it.

Yes, it will hurt. Yes, it will feel like your heart is splintering.

But each step away from what isn't right for you brings you closer to what is. Closer to peace. Closer to clarity. Closer to yourself.

You don't have to settle for crumbs when you were born to feast. You don't have to beg to be seen when the right people will see you effortlessly.

And sometimes, the people who show up for you won't be the ones you expected—but they'll be the ones who were always meant to. And they will show you what kindness looks like. What real connection feels like. What it's like to be loved without conditions, without performance, without fear.

Let go of the people who only loved you in pieces. Let go of the situations that left you more drained than fulfilled. Let go of the version of yourself that stayed quiet, small, and invisible just to be tolerated.

Let go—not because you're weak. But because you're strong enough to start again.

Let go... because freedom is waiting on the other side.

And one day soon, you'll look back and realize: The truth you were so afraid to face... Was actually the key to your healing all along.

✦ ✦ ✦

"Sometimes, the hardest goodbye is the one you give to the version of yourself that kept waiting for love where it was never meant to be found."

Chapter 33

A Language That Found Me

"Sometimes we start something for the wrong reasons
and still end up exactly where we need to be."

I started learning Spanish shortly after my love story with F ended.
To this day, I'm not entirely sure what triggered it. Maybe I was
hoping that, if we ever crossed paths again, I'd impress him somehow.
That maybe he'd see me differently if I spoke his language.

Or maybe... I just needed something new. Something to pour
myself into when everything I believed in had collapsed.

One day, without really planning it, I found myself searching for
tutors online. I signed up for one-on-one Spanish lessons through a
website that connected students with teachers from around the world.

Back then, a part of me still believed F and I would find our way
back to each other—so naturally, I looked for a tutor from Colombia.
I told myself: *If I'm going to learn Spanish, I want it to be the exact*
Spanish he speaks.

I tried many tutors. They were all good—skilled, kind, patient—
but something was missing. I wasn't just looking for a teacher. I was
looking for someone I could click with. Someone I could learn from,
but also talk to. Someone who made the process feel like connection,
not just instruction.

And then I met Sara.

From our very first session, I felt it—an ease. A warmth. A comfort. It wasn't romantic love, but it was love in another form. The kind of love you feel when someone instantly makes you feel seen, safe, and welcome.

I didn't know a word of Spanish then—aside from the basics: *cerveza, hola, buenos días, ¿cómo estás?*—but with Sara, everything felt simple. Exciting. Fun.

She made learning feel like a conversation between two friends instead of a grammar lesson. Slowly, I began to understand. I started recognizing words, piecing together meaning. Eventually, I could follow her even when she spoke only in Spanish. Not every word—but enough to understand the heart of what she was saying.

With time, our relationship evolved. We weren't just teacher and student anymore—we were friends. Once my Spanish improved, our lessons became deeper. More personal. She became not only my language tutor, but in many ways, my therapist too.

I felt safe with her in a way I hadn't felt with many people. I told her about F. About the heartbreak. About everything I was carrying. And she listened—with patience, empathy, and no judgment.

Eventually, I flew to Colombia to meet her. She and her husband welcomed me with open arms. They showed me around, took me out for traditional food, made sure I felt at home in their world.

And I did.

To this day, we're still friends, and I'm endlessly grateful for her presence in my life. Our "lessons" now are more like catch-up calls between two people who genuinely care about each other.

Around the same time, I also connected with another tutor—Alejandro.

From our very first session, we bonded deeply. There was something about him that felt familiar. Easy. Safe. We shared stories, struggles, moments of vulnerability—and supported each other like old friends.

He understood me, and I understood him. We were two souls navigating our own wounds, showing up for each other in the spaces between vocabulary drills and verb conjugations.

To this day, I still talk to both Sara and Alejandro. We laugh, we share, we catch up—sometimes in Spanish, sometimes in Spanglish, always from the heart.

And I am so grateful for meeting them and having them in my life.

What started as a way to maybe impress someone I loved ended up becoming a doorway into a new version of myself.

I fell in love with the language. The way it sounds. The way it moves. The passion it holds in its rhythm. I fell in love with the culture—the joy, the celebration, the warmth of Latin life. I started to understand not just the words, but the soul of the language.

Now I watch Spanish movies without subtitles. I listen to music and understand the lyrics. I can hold conversations, express myself, connect in ways I never imagined.

I'm still learning. I'm still not fluent. But I'm on my way.

And more importantly—I found something I wasn't looking for. I found connection. I found healing. I found friendships that have carried me through some of the hardest days of my life.

Spanish didn't just become a language I could speak. It became a language that helped me feel again.

Learning a new language is so much more than memorizing words or mastering grammar. It's an act of humility. A surrender of ego. A return to curiosity.

It strips you down—reminds you what it feels like to not know. To stumble. To say something wrong and see the confusion flicker across someone's face. To laugh at yourself, or worse, to want to cry because you can't make your mouth match the thought in your head. It's uncomfortable. Vulnerable. Raw. And yet, you keep going.

Because in those awkward pauses, in the silence between broken sentences, something deeper begins to happen. You start to listen differently. You start to notice how tone carries as much as meaning, how gestures fill in the blanks, how kindness can soften even the most butchered phrase. You begin to see the world through different eyes.

Language isn't just communication—it's culture, emotion, history. It's the soul of a people carved into sound. The way someone says *te extraño*—I miss you—in Spanish, carries an ache that English can't quite hold. The way laughter rolls in Latin tongues—round, musical, full-bodied—feels like sunshine. The warmth tucked inside a simple *mi casa es tu casa*—it's not just hospitality. It's an invitation into the heart.

Every word is a doorway. Every phrase a bridge. Every conversation a reminder that language is less about being perfect and more about being willing.

When you open yourself to another language, you open yourself to another way of living, of loving, of being. You learn that there isn't only one way to see the world. And with every word I've learned, I've unlearned a little judgment. With every cultural insight, I've stretched my sense of belonging. With every honest conversation, I've been reminded of the truth we all share: That we are all—at our core—trying to connect. To be understood. To be seen.

Spanish didn't just give me a third language. It gave me friends who taught me patience. Stories that taught me history. Moments that reminded me the most important parts of life can't always be translated.

It gave me a new lens to see the world. Clearer. Softer. Fuller. A lens that showed me that mistakes don't define us, effort does. That vulnerability can be a strength. That connection is always worth the risk of being misunderstood.

And maybe that's the most beautiful part of all: That in trying to understand someone else's language, I finally began to understand more of myself.

✦ ✦ ✦

"Some languages we study to communicate with others. Some find us so we can finally communicate with ourselves."

Chapter 34

A Vacation, A Spark, A Light

*"Sometimes joy doesn't arrive with fireworks or grand
declarations. Sometimes it slips in quietly—through
a stranger's smile, a fleeting spark, or a moment that
feels like sunlight breaking through the cracks."*

I was at the airport with my friend, waiting to board our flight to
Puerto Vallarta—my escape from everything I didn't want to feel.
The place I ran to when I needed to remember what joy felt like. A
place that always welcomed me with open arms, with warmth, laughter, and cobblestone streets that felt like home. Zona Romántica—the
heart of it all. The colors, the charm, the sunsets melting into the ocean
corner like a whispered promise that life could still be beautiful. You
didn't need much more than that to feel alive.

As we waited at the gate, I noticed two guys walking toward us.
One of them caught my eye—and not in some dramatic, slow-motion
way. It was subtle. A flicker. A pull. I looked away. It felt like nothing.
Or maybe it felt like too much.

We boarded soon after. My friend and I had booked separately,
so we weren't seated together. I made my way through the narrow
aisle, scanning rows, and there they were—the same two guys, seated
next to each other with one empty seat beside them. I paused. Could
it really be mine?

It was.

I sat down without saying a word. Neither did they. We shared silence, shared air, shared that strange awareness you get when you feel something but have no idea what it means. I convinced myself they were together. That whatever spark I felt was just me, hoping. So I turned to the window and disappeared into my thoughts.

When we landed, I looked for them, but they were gone. I told myself it was a missed connection. A fleeting, forgettable moment. Life would go on.

But life had other plans.

I found my friend, and we grabbed a cab to our Airbnb. We unpacked just enough to change into swimsuits. Later that day, as we reached the rooftop of our building to catch the last stretch of sun—there they were again. The same two guys. In the same building. In the same city. Under the same fading light. A second chance, gift-wrapped in coincidence.

This time, I said something. We started talking. They had just arrived—it was their first time in Puerto Vallarta. I gave them some tips, told them about the best spots to eat, to dance, to watch the sunset. The conversation was easy, unforced. Like we'd known each other in another life and were just picking up where we left off.

That night, we went out dancing. And somewhere between the music, the heat, and the tequila haze—I saw him again. The one who caught my eye. Christian. Our eyes met across the dance floor. And this time, we didn't look away.

We danced, we talked, we kissed. It was soft, playful. No expectations. Just presence.

We kept running into each other throughout the trip—sometimes by accident, sometimes because one of us made it happen. But our paths kept crossing like the universe was stitching our timelines together. And slowly, something began to grow. Not a relationship. Not a romance. Something harder to name.

When we got back to New York, we stayed in touch. We started seeing each other, talking, hanging out. At first, I thought maybe this would turn into something more—something romantic. There was definitely attraction, chemistry. We kept spending time together—but that initial heat faded. It didn't disappear completely, but it transformed into something quieter.

The more time we spent together, the more I realized—this wasn't about falling in love with him. It was about remembering how to love life again.

He was younger, brighter, softer. Not naïve—just… unguarded. He still believed in people. In possibility. And I hadn't even realized how much I had stopped believing in those things until he walked into my life like sunlight slipping under a locked door. He was younger than me, but in him, I saw something I had lost in myself—a softness. A light. That spark that once made me love the world with wonder, before life dimmed it. He reminded me of who I used to be.

We never defined what we were. There was no need. We just kept showing up. To movies. To messy conversations and late-night laughter. We played chess, and he beat me every time we played. We watched TV and ate strawberries. We shared childhood stories, heartbreaks, favorite snacks. We laughed until our stomachs hurt.

And I found myself falling for him—but not the way I expected. I wasn't falling in love with him. I was falling in love with his energy. His optimism. His vulnerability. The way he talked about life with wide eyes and an open heart.

And I started to feel lighter. Not because he saved me. But because being around him reminded me of who I used to be—before I was hurt, before I was hardened. He helped me rediscover the softness I thought I had lost forever.

I didn't want to possess him. Or label it. I just wanted to protect his light. I wanted him to stay joyful in a world that so often teaches us to dim ourselves just to survive. I wanted to make sure he was safe and happy in this big, new city he was learning to call home.

What I thought was a summer romance turned into something else entirely—a quiet, beautiful friendship. The kind that doesn't demand, doesn't perform, doesn't promise forever… but somehow, still stays.

It was love, but not the kind that breaks you. It was the kind that builds you. That reminds you that joy still exists in the world. That you can still smile even when your heart has been shattered before.

Not all love stories end in heartbreak. Some don't end at all—they just become part of your heart in a different way.

Not every person who enters your life is meant to stay forever. Some come in only to hand you something sacred. A new perspective. A forgotten piece of yourself. A spark. A light. And sometimes, what starts as a fleeting moment becomes a lifetime memory.

Christian reminded me that not all love has to hurt. That love can be simple. Joyful. Unexpected. That it doesn't always need to be romantic to be meaningful.

Christian was that for me—a bright, untamed joy. He didn't heal me. But he made the healing feel less lonely. He didn't fix me. But he reminded me I wasn't broken. He didn't stay forever. But he stayed long enough to leave something permanent in me.

We still talk. We still see each other. And I still smile every time I get a text from him. Because no matter how long it lasts, when someone brings light into your life—you never forget it.

Christian was never mine. But he was meant for me. Even if just for that season. Even if just to remind me… That joy still exists. That people can still surprise you. That your heart still works—even after it's been shattered.

✦ ✦ ✦

"Some people come into your life like summer storms—unexpected, vivid, unforgettable. Not to stay, but to wash the dust from your soul and remind you how to feel again."

Chapter 35

Pink Dragon

"There are friends, there is family, and then there are friends who become family."

For Marie—my pink dragon. The one who reminded me that strength can be soft, that laughter can be healing, and that friendship, when real, survives anything. Thank you for being my light.

There are people in our lives we've known forever who still feel like strangers—and then there are strangers we've just met who feel like home. They understand us, hear us, and see us in ways that feel almost unreal. Not many people can do that. And when you find someone who can, you hold onto them. You cherish them.

As Tom Ford once said: *"When you find somebody good, keep them in your life."*

And I found someone good—really good. Or maybe she found me. Either way, we found each other. She became my pink dragon.

You're probably wondering what that means. Don't worry—I'll explain.

One day, I got a message from a Facebook friend, Tyler. We'd been online friends for years—neither of us even remembered how we met. He wrote: *"My bestie is moving to New York soon. I know it's easy to meet people there, but I think you two need to connect. She's a powerhouse."*

So I said yes. *"Sure. Give her my number."*

A few days later, an unknown number texted: *"Hey, this is Marie. I got your number from Tyler. Want to meet this weekend?"*

It was Pride weekend, and honestly, the last thing I wanted was to meet some random straight girl. So I responded: *"Sorry, I'm busy this weekend, it's Pride! But next week works."*

She didn't hesitate. *"Sure, let me know when and where."*

I suggested Medi, a wine bar just a few blocks from my place. She agreed—Thursday at 7 PM.

Thursday came. It was hot, humid, and raining. I was grateful she was coming to me because I wouldn't have gone far to meet someone I didn't know.

But she came. From Chelsea. In the pouring rain.

And from the moment we said hello, something clicked. It was effortless. We laughed, drank wine, talked about everything and nothing. It felt like we'd known each other for years. Like we were old friends catching up. Like soulmates.

I felt lucky—so lucky. She was funny, smart, confident, effortless. She glowed. And I knew—this was someone who was going to change my life.

Midway through dinner, she asked how I knew Tyler. *"Burning Man?"* she guessed. *"No,"* I laughed. *"We've never met in person. Just Facebook."*

She nearly choked on her wine. *"Wait—he set me up with a stranger? You could've been a serial killer!"* *"Why would I kill you? What would I even do with the body?"*

We both burst into laughter. And that's when our friendship deepened. With laughter. With wine. With honesty.

We started spending more time together. Effortlessly. I introduced her to my friends, and of course, they loved her. Everyone did. She introduced me to hers.

She was different—in the best way. Strong yet kind. Funny yet mature. Smart yet goofy. She was my kind of girl. And I was her kind of guy. We were made for each other—just not in the romantic sense. We were soul friends.

Diamonds, Mimosas, and Puppies

One Sunday, we were out for brunch in the West Village, sipping mimosas and soaking up the chaos of the city. Marie wanted to see an antique ring she'd fallen in love with online. *"You should get it,"* I said. *"You deserve it. You've worked hard for it."*

We may have had one too many drinks, but we were high on joy. Somewhere along the walk to the jewelry shop, I mentioned how badly I wanted a dog—especially a Cavalier King Charles Spaniel, the breed I had once loved and lost.

"If I'm getting that ring," she said, *"you're getting that dog."* I laughed. *"Okay."*

We stopped at a pet store, but there were no King Charles pups that day. So we walked to the jewelry shop instead. And there it was— the ring. An old-cut diamond surrounded by green emeralds. It was stunning. Regal. Fierce. Just like her.

With a little push from me (and another friend), she bought it. Because she deserved it. That ring wasn't just jewelry. It was a crown for a queen who had earned every gem on it.

A few weeks later, COVID hit. Isolation began. All we had was texting and phone calls. And then, out of nowhere, she sent me a photo of the most adorable puppy I'd ever seen. *"I'm getting him,"* she said. *"Where? How?"*

She found him online, in Florida. No overthinking. No waiting. Just doing. That's Marie. Two days later, the puppy—Louie—was home.

Weeks passed. Spring arrived. We met in Bryant Park. I finally met Louie. He was perfect. I held him. He peed on me.

Marie laughed. *"You're his dad now. He marked you!"*

And just like that, I was a dad. She had her diamonds. I had my dog—well, sort of. We shared custody. It became our thing.

Louie was joy in fur. A tiny bundle of happiness.

One afternoon, she casually told me, *"I'm moving back to Denver. I bought a house."* *"What? When? How?"* *"I had a friend FaceTime me the house. I bought it."*

Of course she did. That's Marie. I didn't want her to go. But I knew distance wouldn't break us.

She moved. I visited. She gave me a room in her new home. I brought gifts—for her and for Louie. One of the toys was a pink stuffed dragon.

Louie loved them all. But the pink dragon? That one was special. It became his favorite. And later, the only one he didn't destroy. The last standing, the survivor, Pink Dragon.

That's when the pink dragon became a symbol. A symbol of resilience. Of joy. Of surviving life's chaos. Of never giving up.

Marie became my pink dragon. Because that's what she is.

Strong. Rare. Unapologetically herself. Beautiful in ways that aren't always easy to explain.

A pink dragon is someone who shows up when you least expect them, but most need them. Someone who sees you—really sees you—and doesn't flinch. Someone who becomes a mirror, a cheerleader, a sister, and a force of nature all in one.

Marie became that for me.

She was—and still is—my inspiration. My anchor. My safe place. She stood by me when I was broken, lost, alone. She stayed when others didn't. She loved me unconditionally. She reminded me what true friendship looks like.

True friendships are rare—not because people are rare, but because honesty, consistency, and unconditional love are. Marie showed me what it means to be seen. To be held, emotionally. To be reminded that I matter—not for what I do or give, but just for being me.

She reminded me that we don't have to go through life alone. That sometimes the best people arrive without warning. And when they do, we owe it to ourselves to hold them close.

Sometimes life doesn't give us what we want—it gives us what we need.

I didn't know I needed Marie until she arrived. I didn't know how much I craved that kind of friendship until I was wrapped in it. Her presence reminded me that love isn't only romantic, that soulmates can come as best friends, and that real connection doesn't require explanation—it just is.

The pink dragon didn't survive because it was the strongest. It survived because it was loved. It survived because someone chose it again and again. Just like Marie chose me. Just like I chose her.

And maybe that's the lesson: Resilience isn't always about fighting harder. Sometimes it's about being seen, about being loved for exactly who you are. That's what gives us strength. That's what keeps us going.

There are moments in life when you realize someone didn't just walk into your life—they walked into your soul. That's what Marie did.

She didn't just become a friend—she became a reflection of who I wanted to be. Sometimes it comes as a person who sees through all your masks, your brokenness, your doubt—and chooses you anyway.

She showed me that strength isn't always loud. Sometimes, it's a quiet kind of power—the way someone stays. The way they believe in you when you don't. The way they show up, again and again, without needing anything in return.

Marie taught me that joy can exist in the middle of pain. That laughter can live beside grief. That even when life is falling apart, there are people who will sit in the rubble with you—and remind you of who you are.

She became my anchor when I felt adrift. My mirror when I couldn't see myself. My inspiration when I felt like giving up. And above all, she became my home in a world that often felt unfamiliar.

If you're reading this and thinking about your own "pink dragon"—hold onto them. And if you haven't found them yet, believe that you will.

Life has a way of bringing the right people to us when we least expect it—especially when we're not even sure we deserve it. But I've learned we all deserve that kind of love. That kind of friendship. That kind of safety.

So to Marie—thank you. For every laugh, every tear, every shared silence, every spontaneous adventure. For your unwavering kindness. For your strength. For your softness. For reminding me that I am not alone.

And to the reader: I hope you find your pink dragon. But more importantly—I hope you become one.

Because in this world, we need more people who choose love without conditions, who show up without fear, who inspire simply by being exactly who they are.

That's what Marie did for me. That's what I hope this chapter does for you.

✦ ✦ ✦

"True friendship doesn't just survive the storms—it becomes the shelter."

Chapter 36

Mirror Wars

*"The loudest wars are not fought on battlefields
but in the silence of mirrors—where our reflection
becomes both the enemy and the hope."*

The hardest battles are often the ones no one sees.

There's a quiet war happening every day—inside mirrors, beneath filters, behind glowing screens.

Most people won't see it. But many of us feel it.

It's the war between who we are... and who we think we're supposed to be.

I've fought that war. Still do, some days. And I know I'm not alone.

We live in a world where comparison is constant. Where curated perfection is praised. Where likes and followers seem to define our value. Where the pressure to look better, be better, appear better—never ends.

But behind every flawless photo is a real person, often quietly falling apart.

This is my story. One of identity, body image, self-worth—and the journey back to myself.

We live in a world where social media has become inescapable. It creates, it connects, it entertains... but it also destroys.

We scroll through Instagram or TikTok, watching other people's lives, comparing ours to theirs. Their bodies. Their homes. Their relationships. Their smiles.

Scroll after scroll, it begins to feel real. We lose track of where the screen ends and our lives begin. We forget who we are, and start living in the version of life we *think* we should have.

We become products of social media. Victims. Slaves.

We stop living for life. We start living for likes.

People create entire curated worlds online. Worlds that look brighter, kinder, better.

And slowly, we start measuring our worth against them. Likes become proof we're enough. Silence becomes proof we're not.

We believe the lie that our value can be reduced to numbers. That if we're not popular, rich, beautiful, or fit enough to go viral—then we are not enough. Not lovable. Not worthy.

So we filter our photos. We fix our flaws. We fake our smiles.

We trade authenticity for acceptance.

We shrink. We shape-shift. We lie.

All to feel like we matter.

I know this because I lived it. I still live it sometimes.

I became desperate for those likes, those followers. I wanted to be seen. I wanted to matter.

I filtered my pictures. I edited my body. I starved myself for approval I never really received.

I thought: *If I looked like the fitness models I followed—young, ripped, perfect—maybe then I'd feel good enough. Maybe then, people would accept me.*

But I've always struggled with my body. With self-acceptance. With self-love.

Growing up, I wasn't the best-looking. I wasn't the most popular. I didn't have the "perfect" body. I was chubby. I was teased. And I was gay. That was enough to make me a target. Enough to make me feel wrong before I even understood why. Kids can smell difference, and they made sure I knew it. Every joke, every glance, every whisper was a reminder that I didn't belong.

I carried silent guilt for being different. Like I had done something wrong just by existing. Like my body was proof of my failure. Like being me was a flaw.

So I punished myself. I skipped meals. I starved myself until the hunger felt like a constant reminder that maybe I was fixing what was broken. I chewed gum to keep my mouth busy. I bought diet pills that made me shake, sweat, and hate myself more. I rubbed on slimming creams, as if magic could erase what I thought made me unworthy. I believed every lie that whispered: *"If you just shrink enough, maybe then you'll finally be lovable."*

But I didn't feel lovable. I didn't feel better. I just felt emptier. Hollow. Fragile. Invisible.

That was when the eating disorders and the cycle of shame began.

Food became my prison and my escape. At the top of the roller coaster, I starved myself—counting every calorie, terrified that one bite would undo me. I measured worth by how little I ate, how much I could deny myself. Hunger became my twisted badge of honor.

And at the bottom, I binged. Food became the one thing that didn't judge me, the one comfort I could reach for. Pizza. Popcorn. Chocolate. Ice cream. I'd eat until I was sick, stuffing the emptiness down with every bite. And for a moment—just a moment—I felt full. I felt comforted. I felt quiet inside.

But then the moment passed, and all that was left was disgust. Shame that wrapped around me like a second skin. Self-hatred that screamed louder than hunger ever could.

And I hid it all. I became an expert at pretending. At smiling while I was breaking. At showing up while I was crumbling. No one knew. I never told anyone. I couldn't. The shame was too heavy. Too ugly. Too loud.

So I carried it alone. I lived in the shadow of shame for years.

I developed body dysmorphia so deep it rewired my brain. No matter what the mirror showed, it was never good enough. If I lost weight, I still saw fat. If I gained muscle, I still saw weakness. If I dressed up, I still saw ugly. Every reflection was a distortion, every glance in the mirror another wound.

Too fat. Too thin. Too ugly. Too much. Never enough.

And then came the comparisons—the endless scroll of social media, magazines, ads. Perfect bodies everywhere. Sculpted abs. Flawless skin. Smiles that looked effortless. Lives that looked untouched by shame. And every photo screamed at me: *This is beauty. This is worth. This is what you'll never be.*

The more I scrolled, the smaller I became. The more I compared, the more I disappeared.

I lost confidence. I stopped wanting to be seen. I dodged cameras. I turned my face away from mirrors. I didn't even like my own shadow. I pulled away from people—friends, strangers, anyone—because I couldn't stand the idea of them seeing me the way I saw myself: broken. Disgusting. Unworthy.

That's the thing no one talks about. Body shame isn't just about how you look. It eats your entire life. It strips away your joy. It silences your laughter. It keeps you from living.

I didn't want to be seen. I didn't think I deserved to be. So I hid. And the worst part? A part of me believed maybe that was all I would ever be— a body I hated, a person I couldn't love, a ghost in plain sight.

Even now—after overcoming an eating disorder, after years of healing—I still have days where I look in the mirror and feel not enough. Not good enough. Not beautiful enough. I wish I could say those thoughts disappeared completely. They don't. Some days they still hit me like a punch. Some days I still avoid the mirror because I know what it might tell me.

But I've learned something. I've learned to silence the lies—or at least lower their volume. To stop believing the voices that tell me I need to be someone else to matter. To stop letting social media decide my value like some algorithm could measure my worth.

Because I am enough. I always was. And so are you.

The truth is: we will never be enough for the wrong people. But for the right ones—the ones who love us beyond appearance, status, or perfection—we are always enough. Even at our worst. Especially at our worst.

I've chased approval. I've chased "likes." I've chased validation from people who didn't even know me. And every time, I ended up emptier than before. Because the truth is, fake validation can't fill real wounds. We need to stop chasing fake likes. Stop living for people who shrink us, starve us, silence us. And start valuing the ones who remind us—again and again—that we are worthy just as we are.

Enough is enough. It's time to let the light in. To stop tearing ourselves apart and start learning to piece ourselves back together.

We need to start accepting ourselves. Embracing our differences. Celebrating our uniqueness. We need to stop dimming our light just to fit in. Because every time we make ourselves smaller to be accepted, we betray the very thing that makes us human.

We are enough. Not because of who we follow. Not because of how we look. Not because of how many people "like" us. We are enough... simply because we are.

And there's nothing wrong with wanting to be seen, loved, or celebrated. That's human. That's natural. The danger comes when we start believing we have to *become someone else* to deserve it.

Social media didn't create my insecurities—but it gave them a microphone. It made my doubts louder, my comparisons sharper. It made me forget the most important truth: I don't need to be filtered to be enough.

Healing doesn't happen overnight. It's not linear. It's messy, brutal, exhausting. Some days you take three steps forward, and others you collapse back into old patterns. But it's worth it. Every stumble, every scar, every moment you choose yourself instead of shame—it's worth it.

Every time I choose to show up as me—unfiltered, unedited, unafraid—I reclaim a little more of my power. And so do you.

So if you've ever felt like you're not enough, not beautiful, not seen—please, please remember this: You are enough. Right now. As you are.

You always were. You always will be.

And you don't need to win the war to begin healing. You just need to lay down the weapons— the self-loathing, the comparisons, the starving, the binging— and choose, however shaky, to be kind to yourself again.

I had spent years fighting my own reflection. But outside the mirror, the battles weren't any softer.

Because when you hate yourself on the inside, it bleeds into everything. It followed me into my work—where I let people exploit me, where I kept saying yes because I thought my worth was in how much I could sacrifice. It followed me into my relationships—where I confused attention with love, where I accepted crumbs because I didn't believe I deserved the feast. It followed me into intimacy—where I hid my body, flinched at touch, kept the lights off because I couldn't imagine anyone seeing me and not feeling the same disgust I felt.

Self-hatred doesn't just stay in the mirror. It lives in your voice when you apologize too much. It lives in your silence when you want to speak up but don't. It lives in the people you choose, the jobs you accept, the boundaries you fail to set. It convinces you that you don't deserve better—so you stop asking for it.

That's the thing about healing. It's not just about food. Or mirrors. Or numbers on a scale. It's about rebuilding your entire life after years of believing you weren't worth one.

And that's the work I'm still doing. Every day. Learning to choose me. Learning to believe that I deserve more than survival.

Because I do. And so do you.

I had spent years fighting my own reflection. But outside the mirror, the battles weren't any softer. The same voice that told me I wasn't enough in my body followed me into my work, my relationships, my dreams. It haunted me everywhere I went.

Because the hardest truth of all is this: if you don't believe you're enough, nothing on the outside will ever convince you.

✦ ✦ ✦

"You are not the body you edit, the filter you choose, or the number of likes you count. You are the soul beneath it all—and that has always been enough."

Chapter 37

The Grass Is Not Always Greener on the Other Side

"They lived on stages. I lived in the wings. But it was in the quiet after the curtain fell that I finally heard my own voice."

A Story of Sacrifice, Burnout, and Finally Waking Up (But also of hope—and believing in good people)

They say the grass is always greener on the other side. But what they don't tell you is that sometimes that grass is just Astroturf. Pretty. Polished. Lifeless.

For almost two decades, I lived on what looked like the greener side. I worked as a personal assistant, executive assistant, and house manager to the wealthy and powerful—the one percent. Celebrities. Billionaires. People whose names light up headlines and red carpets.

And from the outside, it looked like I had it all. Private jets. Luxury hotels. Five-star restaurants. Backstage passes to a life most people only see on Instagram.

But the truth? The truth was brutal. And no one wants to talk about it.

Behind that glamorous curtain was a life of servitude. A life where I gave and gave and gave… and still, it was never enough. I wasn't living my own life—I was living theirs. My time wasn't mine. My energy wasn't mine. Even my identity didn't feel like mine anymore.

I became the fixer, the cleaner, the invisible shadow who held everything together so they could shine. I learned how to disappear into the background, how to anticipate needs before they were spoken, how to smile through exhaustion. I became fluent in sacrifice—handing over birthdays, holidays, relationships, sleep, and pieces of myself just to keep the machine running.

I was always on call. Always reachable. I couldn't take a real vacation. I couldn't enjoy holidays. I couldn't even turn off my phone at night, because I lived in fear of missing a call—and being blamed. I wasn't a person anymore. I was a function. A tool. An extension of someone else's convenience.

They didn't care if it was 3 a.m. They didn't care if I was sick, grieving, burned out, or barely surviving. If they needed something— even the most absurd, unnecessary thing—it was my job to fix it. And if I didn't answer fast enough? If I made one small mistake? I wasn't just reprimanded—I was disposable.

I've been blamed for things I had no control over. Missed flights, despite arranging cars hours ahead. Bad weather. Fully booked restaurants I was somehow expected to conjure into availability.

With time, everything became my fault. And the worst part? I started to believe it.

I shrank. I bent. I broke. I told myself: Maybe if I just work a little harder, they'll finally appreciate me. Maybe if I stay quiet, stay late, stay on… they'll see my worth.

They didn't. They never did. They only saw what I didn't do—not the thousands of things I did.

Because when you work for people who believe money gives them power, they start to believe it gives them ownership. Of your time. Your energy. Your soul. You stop existing as a human being. You become something they use.

And when they're done using you, or you say something they don't like, or they wake up and "don't feel it"—you're gone. Just like that. You become a thing. A replaceable part. Someone who knows everything about them, who lived in their shadow, who made sure they had everything they wanted before they even asked. You know their secrets. You've seen their vulnerabilities. And still—you are disposable.

It happened to me. After months of struggling—broke, exhausted, clinging to hope—I finally landed a job that seemed promising. Then, out of nowhere, another offer came in. Flashier. Richer. A dream on paper. They were persuasive, polished, too good to be true.

I accepted. I sublet my apartment. I packed up my life. I gave them everything.

And one week in? They let me go. "He just didn't feel it."

No reason. No warning. Just… gone.

That one sentence shattered what little stability I had managed to rebuild. Gone was the job. Gone was my home. Gone was the hope that maybe, finally, I was getting back on my feet.

I remember sitting in a borrowed room, staring at the wall, trying to process what had just happened. My phone was still in my hand—screen black, heavy as a brick—because I couldn't put it down. Part of me still expected the call to come back. Maybe they'd changed their mind. Maybe it was all some kind of misunderstanding.

But it wasn't. It was real. And it was brutal.

In that silence, shame crept in. Shame for believing the promises. Shame for uprooting my life so quickly. Shame for needing the job so badly that I ignored the warning signs.

And under the shame—grief. Grief for the years I'd poured into a career that had eaten me alive. Grief for the sacrifices I couldn't get back. Grief for the version of me that still believed loyalty and hard work would be enough.

The world tells you that if you grind hard enough, if you stay loyal, if you give more than anyone else—you'll succeed. But in that moment, I realized the truth: in their world, you could give everything and still be discarded without hesitation.

I wasn't just unemployed. I wasn't just homeless. I was hollow.

And yet, in that hollow space, a quiet voice whispered something I hadn't allowed myself to hear before: *You cannot keep living like this.*

Because sometimes the breaking point isn't the end. Sometimes, it's the beginning.

And that was the moment something inside me cracked open. Not a quiet shift. Not a gentle realization. A break. A shattering. A scream I had swallowed for too many years finally clawing its way out.

I realized I couldn't keep doing this. I couldn't keep sacrificing myself for people who never really saw me. I couldn't keep bending until I broke, just to hold up lives that weren't mine to carry.

I couldn't keep handing my life over to the rich and powerful, hoping they'd see the human behind the service. Because they don't. And they won't. Not when power makes people blind. Not when money convinces them that everything—and everyone—has a price tag.

We are living in a world where work has become a battlefield for our humanity. Where loyalty is one-sided. Where effort is expected, demanded, taken for granted—but rarely, if ever, appreciated. Where people are treated like cogs in a machine. And when those cogs wear down, when they stop spinning as smoothly as before—they're replaced. No ceremony. No gratitude. No pause. Just replaced.

You give your time. Your weekends. Your birthdays. Your health. Your soul.

And for what?

A paycheck that barely covers the therapy you now need to survive the job? A thank you that never comes? A title that sounds glamorous but feels like a leash? A job that will drop you the second you stop saying yes?

This system is broken. It grinds people down. It spits them out. It makes them believe that being endlessly available is the same as being valuable. That silence equals strength. That sacrifice equals success.

But it's a lie. And we need to talk about it. Out loud. Unapologetically. Because too many of us are bleeding quietly behind polished résumés and forced smiles. Too many of us are breaking under the weight of expectations that were never human to begin with.

We are not robots. We are not tools. We are not disposable.

We are human beings—with lives, with hearts, with dreams. With families who miss us. With bodies that ache. With spirits that can only bend so far before they snap.

And the moment we start demanding to be treated that way—demanding dignity, respect, humanity—is the moment the grass might finally start growing on our own side. Not painted. Not fake. Not Astroturf. Real. Rooted. Alive.

And for me, that demand started in the smallest way: by saying no. The word I had been terrified to use for years. No, I won't answer your call at 3 a.m. No, I won't sacrifice my health for your convenience. No, I will not keep breaking myself to keep you comfortable.

At first, it felt like rebellion. Like betrayal. Like I was letting someone down. But then I realized—I wasn't betraying anyone. I was saving myself.

I started choosing rest over fear. I started choosing boundaries over burnout. I started choosing my own voice, shaky as it was, over silence.

It wasn't easy. Saying no cost me jobs. It cost me relationships. It cost me the illusion of "security" that had kept me chained to their world for so long. But what I gained was something I hadn't felt in years: freedom.

The freedom to breathe. The freedom to heal. The freedom to be a person again—not just a function.

And maybe that's what this entire journey has been teaching me all along: The greener grass was never out there, on the other side of someone else's fence. It was here. Waiting for me to stop watering everyone else's lawn and finally start tending to my own.

But in all this—there were exceptions. People who restored my faith. People who saw me. People who made all the difference.

I was lucky enough to work for two incredible families—people who welcomed me, trusted me, respected me, and reminded me that goodness still exists.

The first was with Mr. Jones, founder of the legendary rock band *Foreigner*.

It all began with an interview with his manager, Mr. Carson. A legend in his own right—sharp, full of energy, and with a heart as big as his personality. I liked him from the start. He had a way of making people feel at ease, of cutting through the formalities and getting right to the truth of things. Two weeks later, I finally met Mr. Jones.

Our "interview" was barely five minutes long. He was rushing to the airport, bags in hand, half in a hurry but still kind enough to pause. I helped with his luggage, exchanged a few words, and that was it. I walked away not knowing if anything would come of it. That evening, my phone rang. It was Mr. Carson: *"He wants to hire you."*

That moment changed everything. It was the beginning of something rare—something real.

Because I didn't just *work* with Foreigner. I became part of their family.

From day one, they made me feel like I belonged. Not just an employee. Not just a shadow in the background. But part of something larger than myself. Mr. Jones, the entire management team, Mr. Carson, Stewart, Merrie, the band, the crew—everyone opened their hearts to me. They made me feel seen, valued, safe. In a world where I had grown used to invisibility, that feeling was priceless.

And then there was Robin—dear Robin. Their tour manager. He became like a father to me. He took me under his wing when I was still finding my footing. He looked after me, gave me advice, made sure I was okay even when I didn't know how to ask for help. He stood by me in moments when I felt small or overwhelmed.

Robin is no longer with us, and his absence still stings. But his presence never really left. I carry his memory with me everywhere I go. His kindness, his steady guidance, the way he reminded me that I mattered—it lives on inside me.

And I will never forget one of his mottos: *"Trust, but always verify."* Simple words, but they stuck with me. They became a quiet compass—reminding me that faith in people is necessary, but so is wisdom. That it's okay to open your heart, but not at the cost of your clarity.

He is missed beyond words. But his lessons—his voice, his laughter, his wisdom—are stitched into the fabric of who I am.

That job wasn't just a job. It was a home. It was proof that work could be different—that you could serve without losing yourself, that respect and kindness could exist even in an industry built on fame and pressure. It was the rare reminder that, yes, there are still people out there who treat others as human beings first.

And in those years, I learned something I'll never forget: sometimes it only takes one person, one family, one team to remind you of your worth. To remind you that you're not invisible. To remind you that there is goodness left in this world.

The second was with Julian Casablancas of *The Strokes*.

It wasn't always easy. In fact, it was the opposite.

We fought a lot in the beginning. Everything I did seemed wrong. Every attempt I made seemed to fall short. I felt like I was walking on glass—never sure when I'd misstep, never sure what reaction I'd get. He was frustrated. I was frustrated. And for a while, it felt like we were locked in a silent war neither of us really wanted to fight.

But looking back now, I see it differently. It wasn't anger. It was trust being built—slowly, painfully, in the only way it sometimes can be when you've been burned too many times before.

We were learning each other's rhythms. His silences. His moods. His boundaries. His triggers. And my persistence, my patience, my refusal to give up.

Because here's the thing: when you're famous—when you're constantly surrounded by people who want something from you—real trust becomes rare. Real friendship, even rarer. Everyone wants a piece of you, and sooner or later, you stop believing that anyone can want *you* for you.

But with time, the walls softened. The sharp edges dulled. The arguments started to fade.

He began to see me. Not as another person on his payroll. Not as a shadow in the background. But as someone who was there for reasons that couldn't be bought.

He began to trust me. To let me in. He knew I wasn't there to take. I was there to give. To support. To care. To protect.

And in that strange, chaotic world of music and fame, that mattered. Because what we built wasn't just professional—it was personal.

Eventually, I wasn't just an assistant. I was a friend.

And though our paths eventually parted, I hope he knows—he always has a friend in me. Someone who will show up. No matter what. Someone who saw him—the human, not the headline.

And maybe that's the biggest gift these rare connections gave me: the reminder that even in the most brutal industries, even in the loneliest rooms, trust and friendship can still grow. Sometimes slowly. Sometimes painfully. But when they do, they leave a mark that never fades.

So yes—there are good people out there. People who see you. Who value you. Who welcome you in and remind you that you are more than your job. Who don't just take what you can give, but give something back—kindness, trust, respect, humanity.

If you haven't found them yet—don't settle. Keep going. Because the wrong places will convince you to shrink, to forget who you are, to believe you're replaceable. But the right places? They will remind you that you are irreplaceable. That you are more than a title, more than your ability to serve, more than what you can sacrifice.

Know your worth. Guard it with everything you have. And walk away from anything—or anyone—that asks you to forget it.

Yes, money matters. Especially in this world. But so does your peace. So does your health. So does your dignity. So does the ability to wake up in the morning and not feel like you've sold your soul for a paycheck that will never be enough.

Go where you're welcomed. Go where you're appreciated. Go where people remember your name, your heart, your effort—not just your usefulness.

Because at the end of the day, the jobs will come and go. The paychecks will be spent. The titles will fade.

But your life? Your soul? Your peace? That's yours. And you don't get another one.

Never, ever settle for less than you deserve. Not in work. Not in love. Not in life.

Because the moment you stop settling, the grass finally begins to grow—real, alive, rooted—on your own side.

✦ ✦ ✦

"The grass may look greener on the other side—but the only grass worth standing on is the one you've grown with your own hands, watered with your own worth, and tended with your own truth."

Chapter 38

My Sanctuary

*"Sanctuary isn't always a place you go to. Sometimes,
it's something you build inside yourself—rep by
rep, breath by breath, moment by moment."*

Sanctuary. It is not always a place. Sometimes, it's the soft silence between heartbeats, the exhale after holding it all in for too long.

Sanctuary is where the world stops asking, and you stop answering. Where you are no longer someone's promise, someone's disappointment, someone's solution.

It's the room you close the door to without guilt. The corner where the light hits just right. The walk in the cold where no one speaks your name. It's the bath where you dissolve. The journal page where you bleed. The moment when your phone is off and your soul is finally on.

It's where your mind can wander without being chased. Where your thoughts are messy—but safe. Where your tears don't need permission, and your joy doesn't need explanation. It's where you can be fragile and whole in the same breath. Where you don't have to hold it all together.

It is where you come home to yourself. Not to be fixed— but to be found.

And through all the sorrow, all the heartbreak, all the noise— I found my sanctuary.

It wasn't a mountaintop or a beach or a quiet cabin in the woods. It was my gym.

That was the place I could breathe. The place I escaped to when everything felt like too much. The one place where I could be with my thoughts, where I didn't have to explain myself, where I could just be.

No masks. No expectations. Just effort.

It gave me purpose. It gave me peace. It gave me progress.

Every day, I go—religiously. Not out of obsession, but out of devotion.

Because it makes me better. Physically, yes. But more than that—it makes me feel alive. It reminds me that I'm capable of showing up for myself, even when no one else does.

And on the days I skip it—when I feel too lazy or too tired—I feel guilty. Because this place is sacred. It's where I grow, where I let go, where I become.

Then I remind myself: I am lucky. I am privileged to have this space. To have a gym close to my home. To have a body that can move. To have a corner of the world where I feel safe, where I feel strong, where I feel like I belong.

It took me a long time to get here. To learn what to do. How to work out. What to eat. How to move without fear of judgment.

In the beginning, I was terrified. I didn't want to look stupid. I didn't want to be seen.

I was the quiet one in the corner, watching others, mimicking movements, hoping no one would notice that I had no idea what I was doing.

But I showed up anyway. Again and again. And little by little, I learned.

About form. About function. About food. About fuel. About discipline. About myself.

Fitness started as a goal, but it grew into something far greater. It became a language my body could speak fluently when my heart was exhausted, when grief, fear, or uncertainty left me without words. It gave me a way to express resilience, to fight back without shouting, and to heal without pretending.

Through sweat and repetition, I discovered something I hadn't felt in a long time: control. Every workout became proof that I could choose progress even when life felt stuck. Fitness became a door that never closed—a space I could always step into when every other path seemed blocked.

I'm still learning, and I want to keep learning. Growth doesn't stop with a stronger body; it deepens with a stronger mind and expands when shared with others. One day, I hope to give back—to take everything I've absorbed and offer it forward.

To help someone else experience what I feel now: Not just strength in their body, but freedom in their soul.

Because fitness isn't only about muscles, routines, or goals. It's about remembering that, no matter how heavy life gets, we can carry more than we ever believed.

And this, too, is love. Not the romantic kind. Not the kind written in movies or whispered in late-night promises. But love, nonetheless.

Love for the body I once hid, the body I once cursed, the body I once thought had failed me. To look in the mirror now and see not shame, but strength— that is love.

Love for the discipline that pulled me out of the dark, for the quiet mornings when I chose to rise instead of hide, for the nights when exhaustion sat heavy on my chest, and still, I showed up. That is love.

Love for the process— for the slow, steady climb, for the setbacks that taught me patience, for the small victories that stitched me back together. Because healing is not a straight road, but every stumble and every step is proof that I kept going.

Love for growth— for the way pain transformed into progress, for the way struggle became strength, for the way effort bloomed into freedom.

This kind of love matters. It anchors us when everything else feels unstable. It gives us purpose when the world grows too loud, when chaos and heartbreak try to drown us out. It reminds us we're still here, still capable, still becoming.

It pushes us through the worst days and whispers that we are not done yet. That we matter. That we are not invisible. That every drop of sweat, every choice to keep going, is a quiet revolution.

And maybe—just maybe— that's what sanctuary really is. Not a place we find outside of ourselves, but the space we create within.

The place where we meet the best version of who we are becoming— not all at once, but slowly, steadily, one rep, one breath, one moment at a time.

✦ ✦ ✦

"Sanctuary isn't always found in silence or solitude. Sometimes, it's found in sweat, in effort, in the quiet promise we make to ourselves to keep showing up—especially when no one's watching."

Chapter 39

Mother Ayahuasca: The Call Back to Myself

"Sometimes the only way forward is not to escape the darkness, but to walk straight into it—because that's where the truth waits."

I was unraveling. Still full of grief. Still full of pain. Still trapped in the quiet chaos of everything I had lost—my job, my health, my relationships, my confidence, my sense of self. Everything around me was falling apart. But worse than that... everything inside me was, too.

I was searching for something—anything—to hold onto. A reason. A direction. A light. Someone to look me in the eyes and say, *"It's going to be okay."* But no one did. And deep down, I wasn't sure I'd believe them even if they had.

One night, I was lying in bed, numb and exhausted, doing what I always did when I didn't know what else to do—mindlessly scrolling through Instagram. Quote after quote, post after post, trying to find something that would make me feel less alone, less lost, less broken.

I wasn't looking for anything in particular. I just needed something to make the heaviness inside me make sense.

And then—I found it. A page appeared. A post. A name.

Arkana Spiritual Center.

Something about it made me stop. I clicked. I started reading.

Arkana was a spiritual healing center with locations across South America and Mexico—but one retreat was different. Remote. Deep in the Peruvian jungle. Far from noise. Far from distractions. Far from the world that had broken me.

They worked with something called Mother Ayahuasca. A sacred medicine. A teacher. A spirit.

As I read more, something in me stirred. This wasn't a vacation. This wasn't an escape. This was something else. Something ancient. Something holy.

And without thinking, without waiting, without second-guessing—I booked a spot. One week in the Amazon jungle. I didn't even know what I was fully walking into. All I knew was that something deep inside me whispered: *"Go."*

The Journey to the Jungle

The journey to Arkana felt surreal from the very beginning. I flew to Lima, Peru… then to Iquitos. From there, a two-hour ride along the Amazon River, followed by a three-hour boat trip into the jungle itself.

The river was breathtaking. Massive. Majestic. Alive. The water was wide and wild—both beautiful and dangerous. It pulsed with energy, like a living thing. It was life and death in the same current. Powerful. Untamed. Sacred.

As the boat carried us deeper into the jungle, I sat quietly, watching the trees blur past, the sounds of nature getting louder, and the world I knew growing further behind me.

This was it. No turning back.

For as long as I could remember, I had dreamed of the jungle. Of the Amazon. Of disappearing into something ancient and untouched. And now… I was here. The dreams do come true.

Headed toward a place with no Wi-Fi, no mirrors, no distractions. A place where healing wasn't sold—it was earned. Where people from all over the world gathered not to escape life, but to finally face it. To cry, to remember, to surrender. To sit with themselves—fully, honestly, painfully.

And I was one of them. One of the broken ones. The searching ones. The brave ones. Hoping that somewhere deep in that jungle, surrounded by strangers and shamans and spirits, I would find something I hadn't felt in a long time... peace. Or maybe, if I was lucky—myself.

The Opening Circle

Before we were allowed to drink the medicine, we had to do something that, for me, was even scarier—we had to speak. We sat in front of the shamans, one by one. We had to tell them why we came. What we were looking for. What we wanted from Mother Ayahuasca.

It felt like standing before a divine council—like they were seeing every part of our souls without needing to ask a single question. It felt like sitting in front of judges who could weigh your entire life in silence.

But there was no judgment. Only presence. Stillness. Peace.

And yet, I was terrified. Because for the first time in my life, I had to say the truth out loud. And that... that was the scariest part.

I had spent my entire life holding things in, swallowing my pain, softening my voice. Afraid that if I spoke too much or showed too much, I would lose the people I loved. And now, I was being asked to speak—to say out loud what I had never dared to.

And so I did. With a shaky voice and a breaking heart, I said: *"I want to come home to myself."*

Why I Needed Mother Ayahuasca

Back then, I didn't know how to explain it. Why I kept searching. Why I kept running toward chaos and calling it clarity.

But now I know. I was looking for a way back to myself.

For those who don't know, Ayahuasca isn't a drug. It's a teacher. A sacred plant medicine used for centuries by Indigenous healers in the Amazon. A brew made from two plants—the Ayahuasca vine and the Chacruna leaf—combined to unlock something most people spend their entire lives avoiding: truth.

They call her "Mother" because she doesn't come to you gently. She comes to show you what you've buried. To bring the hidden parts of you to the surface. To sit you down with your demons, your grief, your wounds, your lies—and say, *"Look. You don't get to run from this anymore."*

Ayahuasca breaks you open. Not to hurt you, but to heal you. She shows you the parts of yourself you abandoned. She takes you into the dark so you can remember your own light. She doesn't care about your mask, your achievements, or your Instagram smile. She wants your truth. All of it. Even the parts you're afraid to admit exist.

And I was ready. I needed it. Because deep down, I knew I was carrying too much. Too much heartbreak. Too many memories. Too many versions of myself I no longer recognized.

I didn't just want a reset. I wanted rebirth.

The First Ceremony

That night, we gathered in the maloka, the ceremonial hut. A wide circular space with wooden floors and a thatched roof, surrounded by candles and silence. Mats lined the edge of the circle. Buckets placed beside each one—because Ayahuasca doesn't just purge the soul, it purges the body too.

I was nervous. I was hopeful. I was terrified.

The brew was thick, dark, earthy. It smelled like smoke and soil and something ancient. When it was my turn, I took it with shaking hands. Closed my eyes. Whispered a silent prayer I didn't even know I still believed in.

And drank.

It burned. Not like fire—but like memory. Bitter, deep, unfamiliar. And then I waited.

The first hour was quiet. I lay on my mat, staring at the ceiling, heart pounding. *Is it working? What if nothing happens? What if something does?*

Then… it began.

The room began to breathe. The jungle grew louder. The candles flickered like they were watching me. And then came the visions. Not dreams. Not hallucinations. Truths.

Mother Ayahuasca didn't come as a woman. She came as a feeling. A presence. She wrapped around me like fog—everywhere and nowhere—and whispered truths I had spent my life trying not to hear.

"You are tired of performing."

I cried. Not soft, pretty tears. But guttural, messy sobs. My body shook. My heart ached. I couldn't hide, not even from myself.

Then came the purge.

I reached for the bucket and everything I had been holding in—emotionally, spiritually, physically—came out of me. Pain I didn't even know I was still carrying poured from my body. It felt violent. And yet... it felt like mercy.

No one came to comfort me. No one held my hand.

And I realized something: this was mine to go through. No one could walk this part for me. I wasn't there to be saved. I was there to see.

The ceremony lasted all night. I saw people crying, screaming, laughing. Some lay still in silence. Each person was in their own universe, their own journey. But somehow, we were all doing it together. All returning to the parts of ourselves we had long forgotten.

As the sky began to lighten and the jungle softened into morning, something in me shifted. I had survived my first night with her. Mother Ayahuasca had shown me just enough to open a door—not to a place, but to myself.

And I knew this was just the beginning.

The Second Descent

The morning after felt like waking up after a storm you survived—but barely. I didn't feel healed. I didn't feel new. I felt... emptied. Quiet. Shaken. Soft.

Integration, they called it. But it felt more like floating. Like my soul hadn't fully returned to my body yet.

That night, we prepared for ceremony number two.

I thought I was ready. But you're never really ready.

You walk into that maloka knowing the medicine will find whatever you're hiding. And she doesn't knock. She kicks the door in.

This time, it didn't take long.

The visions came quicker. More intense. No warm-up. No easing in.

I saw my past. But not the version I remembered—the version I had avoided.

I saw myself as a child, hiding under the table during arguments. I saw the first time I learned that love meant keeping quiet to be safe. I saw every time I shrank myself to make someone else comfortable. Every time I said *"I'm fine"* when I wasn't. Every time I begged for love with my silence.

It crushed me.

But then, something shifted.

She didn't just show me pain. She showed me strength. How I survived. How I kept showing up for others, even when no one showed up for me. How I smiled through it all.

"You were never too much," she said. *"You were too alone."*

And that broke me in a way nothing ever had.

Because that was the wound I kept avoiding—not the heartbreak. Not the rejection. But the loneliness.

The deep, quiet ache of trying to be worthy in a world that made me feel like I wasn't.

And in that moment, something inside me softened.

I held myself. Not metaphorically—literally. I curled into a ball on my mat and held my own body the way I had always needed someone to. And I wept.

Not for others. For me.

That night, I didn't purge. But emotionally? Spiritually? I let go of so much.

And when the sun began to rise, I didn't feel empty anymore. I felt... real. Not healed. Not finished. But real.

The Third Ceremony – The Roller Coaster

By the third night, I thought I knew what to expect. But Mother Ayahuasca isn't predictable.

The vision started beautifully. Like a dream. I felt like I was on a roller coaster—colors swirling around me, deep and bright. I felt happy. Peaceful.

And then... the cart began to move faster.

Too fast.

Voices started to chase me. Then came the creatures—human-like but faceless, with long monkey arms. They screamed, threw things at me, blew smoke in my face.

They got closer. And closer. Touching me. I could hear them so loud, I could feel them.

The smoke filled my lungs. I couldn't breathe. It was overwhelming.

So intense it felt like reality.

And just when I thought I couldn't take it anymore—

It all stopped.

Darkness. Complete stillness.

I thought I had failed. But I hadn't. Because later, I understood—she had shown me what I needed to see.

The vision that repeats until you finally understand its meaning.

And I understood now.

The Fourth Ceremony – Stillness

The final ceremony felt different from the start. The maloka was quieter. The jungle was still.

Some people cried. Others laughed.

I felt peace.

There were no visions. No chaos. No terror.

Just breath. Just presence.

She let me rest. She had already shown me what I needed to see.

That I wasn't broken. Just buried. That I had always been worthy. That I didn't need to prove anything anymore.

I lay under the stars, in the middle of the Amazon jungle, and listened: to the river, to the shamans, to my own breath.

And for the first time in a long time, I felt like I belonged.

Not to someone else. Not to a dream. Not even to healing.

But to myself.

I came to the jungle searching for healing. I left with something even more precious—truth. Not the kind you read about or hear from someone else, but the kind you feel deep in your bones. The kind you earn through surrender.

Ayahuasca didn't give me answers. She gave me myself.

She showed me my shadows, my pain, my resilience, and my worth. She stripped away the masks I wore, the stories I told, the lies I believed. And beneath it all, she handed me something I had forgotten how to hold:

Peace.

Not the peace of everything being perfect, but the peace of knowing I don't have to run anymore. That I am allowed to be soft. That I am allowed to speak. That I am allowed to be seen.

And now, I carry her with me—not as a memory, but as a mirror. A reminder that I am my own medicine.

And that maybe, just maybe, I always was.

✦ ✦ ✦

"Healing didn't come in light. It came in darkness. It came when I stopped running, when I faced myself, and when I finally whispered, 'I forgive you.'"

Chapter 40

They Didn't Have to—But They Did, Because They Chose Love

"The purest acts of love are the ones that are never required, yet given anyway."

There's so much love in this world. But not all love is romantic. Not all love comes dressed in roses and promises.

Sometimes, we spend so long searching for one kind of love that we miss the thousands of other ways it's already surrounding us.

Sometimes, love is quieter. Sometimes, it comes in unexpected forms—in the loyalty of friends, in the embrace of family, in the way a stranger shows up when it matters most.

Love is everywhere. If we open our eyes—really open them—we'll see it.

There's the love we receive from our families—the people who raised us, fought with us, forgave us, and stood by us even when it was hard.

There's the love of true friends—the ones who remind us of our worth when we've forgotten.

There's the love we feel for animals, for the earth, for art, for music, for food, for people—all kinds of people.

And then there are people who use their voice, their power, their influence, and their wealth to help others—people who could've stayed silent, but didn't. Who could've lived comfortably, but chose to show up. They give their time, energy, and resources to create change—to protect, to uplift, to heal. They don't wear capes, but they are heroes. They use what they have not to flaunt power—but to empower others.

These are the people who've inspired me. People who helped me heal. People who reminded me that you don't have to be perfect to make a difference—you just have to care enough to try.

Kim Kardashian and the Kardashian Family. I know people criticize them—for their lifestyle, their spending, their fame, the glamour, the extravagance. But beneath all of that, I saw something else. I saw family. I saw loyalty. I saw love.

The truth is: they worked for what they have. They built an empire—together. And at the center of it all was family.

For a long time, I didn't see that. I judged them, too. But when I started watching their show, something in me shifted.

I saw how they showed up for each other—through heartbreaks, through fights, through public scrutiny. No matter what, they always came back to each other. They aren't perfect—but they are real. And they always, always stand by their family.

Kim, especially, inspires me. She didn't have to go back to school. She didn't have to study law. She didn't have to fight for justice.

But she did.

She chose to stand beside those forgotten by the system. She fights for criminal justice reform. She speaks up for immigrants. She uses her name, her platform, her status—to challenge what's broken. She gives a voice to those the world has ignored.

And she doesn't have to. But she chooses to. And that matters.

Thank you, Kim—for being more than what the world expected. For showing us that luxury and justice can live side by side. For proving that power and purpose can coexist.

Bethenny Frankel. Bethenny shows up. Again and again.

When disaster strikes, she's not on a red carpet—she's on the ground.

When Puerto Rico was devastated by a hurricane—before the government responded—Bethenny was already there. When floods hit Texas, when war broke out in Ukraine—she showed up. Not for show. Not for clout. But with food. With money. With compassion. With action.

Her foundation, BStrong, has done more for some communities than the systems that were supposed to protect them.

She didn't have to be there. But she chose to.

Bethenny, thank you—for standing in the gap. For being there when others weren't. For being the definition of what it means to lead with heart.

Lady Gaga & Madonna. These women have always stood with us—loudly, unapologetically, and without hesitation.

They've supported the LGBTQ+ community not just when it was popular—but when it was dangerous. When it was radical. When it mattered most.

When governments failed us—they didn't. When the world told us to be quiet—they sang louder.

They made us feel seen. They gave us strength.

So many gay men I know—including myself—owe part of our survival to them. Their music, their voices, their presence helped us make it through.

They gave us permission to exist. To be proud. To feel beautiful in a world that told us we weren't enough.

They've supported us from the beginning. And they still do. Not because they have to. But because they choose to.

And for that, I will always be grateful.

Oprah. Oprah is a global symbol of wisdom, strength, and compassion.

She poured her soul into lifting others—through stories, through truth, through hope. She reminded people that they are not their past. That they can rise. That they can dream beyond survival.

She's healed, inspired, and guided generations—including mine.

Thank you, Oprah—for your grace, your voice, and the light you continue to share with the world.

Andy Cohen. Andy brings joy to our community.

He makes us laugh. He creates space for real conversations. He reminds us that we're allowed to take up space.

But what I admire most is the beautiful family he built.

As a single gay man, he chose fatherhood. He created a home full of love, stability, and joy—all on his own. That takes heart.

You don't need a traditional love story to build a beautiful family. And Andy is living proof of that.

I don't know if he's found romantic love—and if he has, I'm happy for him. If not, I hope it finds him soon. He deserves it.

Thank you, Andy—for showing us what strength looks like. For using your voice to advocate for LGBTQ+ rights. For showing up—again and again—with pride, with purpose, and with love.

Steve Irwin. Steve Irwin was my childhood hero.

His love for animals, for nature—for life—was real and contagious. Watching him made me feel connected to the world in a deeper way.

He taught us to respect life in all its forms.

He left this world too soon, but his legacy lives on through his children, especially his son, who carries that same spark.

Steve reminded us that passion is powerful. And that love for the earth is one of the purest kinds of love there is.

Thank you, Steve—for all that you gave us. We still feel it. We still remember.

All of these people—flawed, human, imperfect—chose to do something with what they had. They used their voice. Their status. Their influence. Their power. To help. To heal. To stand up.

They didn't have to. But they did.

And I see that. And I'm thankful.

Because they made me feel seen. They helped me believe I could do something too—that maybe, one day, I could use my voice to make a difference.

We live in a world that is so quick to cancel, to criticize, and to point fingers. But maybe we should spend more time lifting up the ones who show up. Even when they don't have to.

No one is perfect. We all have a past. We all carry regrets.

But we grow. We learn. We become.

Let's stop expecting perfection—from ourselves, or anyone else. Let's focus on who we're becoming. Let's forgive. Let's let go. Let's rise.

Because we all started somewhere. And when we rise, we have a chance to lift others.

One person at a time. One act of kindness. One voice of hope.

There's a beautiful song written in memory of the Orlando shooting victims. It's called *Hands*. And one of the lyrics says:

"Hands, they can love or they can take. They can fight until they save. They can break the world—or they can change it too."

"Doesn't matter who you love. All that matters is you love."

And it's true.

Our hands can destroy. But they can also rebuild. Our voices can tear down. But they can also uplift. Our hearts can close. But they can also open.

We get to choose.

Let's choose love. Let's choose softness in a world that teaches us to be hard. Let's be the reason someone still believes in kindness.

Let's use our hands to build—not break. Let's use our voices to heal—not hurt. Let's be gentle. Let's be bold. Let's be love.

Because love is everything. Love is the reason we survive. Love is the reason we keep going.

Because love isn't just romantic. It's how we show up. It's how we care. It's how we give.

And in case no one's told you lately— Your voice matters. Your actions matter. You matter.

Be the light. Be the difference. Be love.

✦ ✦ ✦

"In a world quick to judge, the ones who choose to help—even when they don't have to—are the ones who change it."

Chapter 41

Time to Say Goodbye – Love Letter
to a City That Never Stayed

"I gave New York my years, my energy, my heart—and
it gave me everything, then took some of it back.
Now I'm leaving, not because I stopped loving it, but
because I finally started loving myself more."

New York has been my home away from home for twenty years. The city I fell in love with. The city I cursed under my breath. The city that broke me, rebuilt me, and taught me every shade of emotion in between.

I came here when I was nineteen—barely an adult, still clinging to the innocence of the boy I was in Poland. I left behind everything I knew: the mountains, the familiar streets, the faces that had known me since birth. I traded crisp mountain air for a skyline I had only ever seen on movie screens. In my head, it was going to be magical—bright lights, happy endings, the love of my life waiting just around the corner. I thought I was walking into a story I'd already seen play out in the films that raised me.

But nothing prepares you for the truth of New York. It's intoxicating and exhausting, like falling in love with someone who will never truly be yours. It gives you dreams in one hand and takes them with the other. It's a city of constant motion—love and hate tangled together, hope and heartbreak sharing the same streets.

On the good days, New York is electric. It's the skyline glowing gold at sunset, the hum of a subway car carrying strangers with a thousand different stories, the street musicians who make you stop in your tracks because their song somehow feels like it was meant just for you. It's the smell of roasted chestnuts in winter, the first glimpse of Central Park in full bloom, the way the city comes alive after a summer thunderstorm. It's rooftop laughter, 3 a.m. pizza slices, and the quiet magic of watching snow fall on streets that still keep moving. It's a place where you can reinvent yourself a hundred times and no one will question it—because everyone here is chasing something, and everyone understands the hustle.

But New York has another side. The side that doesn't make the postcards. It's the loneliness you feel while standing in a crowd, the strangers' eyes that slide past you without seeing you. It's the rent that drains your spirit, the jobs that chew up your time and leave you too tired to dream. It's the subway at 2 a.m., where the shadows feel longer and the wrong glance can turn dangerous. It's the sirens that wake you in the middle of the night, the arguments you overhear through paper-thin walls, the quiet tragedies playing out behind apartment doors.

And it's also the city of lonely people—millions of souls moving side by side but never really touching. Here, no one wants to take a chance on love because everyone believes there's always something—or someone—better waiting just out of sight. It's a place where connections spark fast, burn bright, and just as quickly vanish before you can even call them yours.

I still remember stepping out of the airport for the first time—September 16th. The hot, humid air smacked me in the face like a stranger's open palm. I didn't even know what humidity was; in the Polish mountains, even the hottest days carried a clean, sharp breath of air. Here, it felt like I'd been dropped into a boiling pot, struggling to inhale.

My cousin drove me to her apartment in an Orthodox Jewish neighborhood in Brooklyn—a place that felt like it belonged to another century entirely. The streets were quieter there, almost insulated from the city's chaos. Women walked in long skirts and wigs, pushing strollers with two or three children bundled inside, their faces half-hidden beneath sunshades. Men in black suits and wide-brimmed hats hurried past, their side curls—payot—framing faces that never seemed to look directly at you but rather through you, as if the outside world was just background noise.

Shops were small and unassuming, signs written in Hebrew letters, windows crowded with challah bread, jars of pickles, and stacks of kosher goods. On Fridays, just before sunset, the streets would grow busier, but the air would also shift—anticipation mixing with the smell of fresh bread and roast chicken as families prepared for Shabbat. Then, as the sun dipped below the buildings, everything would go still. No cars. No phones. Just people walking slowly, talking softly, the pace of life slowing to something I had never experienced in New York before.

It was a world with its own rules, its own rhythm—one that seemed untouched by the rush and hunger of the city just beyond its borders. And for me, fresh off the plane from the Polish mountains, it was like stepping into a photograph frozen in time. Beautiful in its way, but also alien. I didn't see the skyscrapers I'd dreamed of. I didn't hear the buzz of ambition or the music of the subway. Instead, I was surrounded by a culture I didn't understand, in a language I didn't speak, with traditions that seemed set in stone.

It wasn't the New York I had seen in the movies. It wasn't the New York I thought I was moving to.

And for a nineteen-year-old who had imagined bright lights and romance, it was disorienting—lonely in a way I had never known before. I felt like an outsider looking through a window into someone else's life, unable to open the door. The streets here didn't hum with opportunity for me; they whispered that I didn't belong. Nights felt longer. Days felt heavier. I missed the smell of the mountains after rain, the sound of people calling my name.

But somewhere in that discomfort, a quiet fire began to burn. I told myself I would learn this city. I would find my place in it, even if it took years. I would adjust. I would make it. And I did.

Day by day, I learned the language of this place—not just the words, but the rhythm. The subway screeches that became background music to my mornings. The smell of fresh bagels and burnt coffee drifting from corner carts as the city shook itself awake. The rush of

Times Square at midnight, where the lights were so bright you could almost believe it was still daytime, and the energy in the air felt endless.

I found a favorite pizza place where the waitresses, dear Carmella, knew my order before I spoke. I danced until sunrise in clubs that seemed to exist in a world of their own, then stumbled home with friends, laughing until our sides hurt. I walked the Brooklyn Bridge in the early hours when the city was still wrapped in quiet, and I felt like the whole skyline was mine. Summers were for open-air concerts, lazy afternoons in Central Park, Fire Island, and rooftop bars where you could watch the sun disappear behind the buildings. Winters brought ice skating at Rockefeller Center, watching the tree light up like something from a dream, and snow falling so softly it almost made the city feel gentle.

New York gave me moments that felt cinematic—falling in love under neon lights, late-night conversations on fire escapes, finding a tiny hole-in-the-wall restaurant that served the best food I'd ever tasted. It gave me independence. It gave me courage. It gave me the thrill of knowing that at any given moment, something extraordinary could happen.

I still remember the day I got the keys to my first apartment in Manhattan—Hell's Kitchen. I walked in and cried. I had made it. The boy from the farm was now living in the center of the world. I could feel the pulse of the city in my bones—the taxis honking below, the laughter spilling from bars, the hum of ambition that seemed to seep through the walls. For years, I thrived on it. I fed off the chaos, the possibility, the endless stream of people and stories and chances to be someone new.

But slowly—so slowly I almost didn't notice at first—the magic began to fade. Nights out felt longer, but emptier. Friends started moving away, and the laughter that used to echo in my apartment became rare. The same bright lights that once thrilled me began to feel harsh, almost unkind. The constant noise that used to energize me began to drain me. I noticed how crowded the sidewalks were, but how alone I still felt walking down them. I saw the way people's eyes darted past each other, the way conversations ended before they began.

And that's when I understood—New York doesn't slow down for anyone. It doesn't stop to ask if you're okay. It doesn't hold you when you're tired. It keeps moving, and if you can't keep up, it leaves you behind.

The city hadn't changed—but I had. I hadn't stopped loving the city—it's just that the way we fit together had changed. What once felt like an embrace now felt like a constant push. I had come here to find myself, and I had. But the version of me I am now needs something different. Something softer. Something that stays.

And one day, I realized I wasn't chasing the magic anymore. I was just trying to hold on to it, and it was slipping through my fingers.

This city made me who I am. It gave me everything—then took some of it back. And I will always carry both—the gratitude and the grief.

But New York doesn't feel like home anymore. And I think... I think it's time to say goodbye. Not because I hate it. But because I need air again. I need space. I need a new chapter—one where I can breathe and build without the weight of the past pressing against me.

I don't know where I'm going yet. Maybe Miami, the city that once almost felt like home. Maybe this time it won't be almost. Maybe this time, I'll stop living in maybes altogether. It's time to start writing a new story—one where I am in charge of my happiness, my choices, my life.

And maybe, just maybe... this goodbye will be the beginning I've been waiting for all along.

Which is why it's time to tell you this...

To the City I Loved Like a Person

"You were the great love I could never quite hold.
You dazzled me from the moment I arrived—
your lights, your rhythm, your endless promises.
I chased you like a dream I didn't want to wake from,
and for a while, you let me believe I belonged to you.
But you were never mine.
You belonged to everyone, and no one at all.
You kissed me with opportunity,
then left me standing alone in the cold.

You kept me hungry—
for more, for better, for something just out of reach.
You made me fall in love with strangers I'd never see again.
You taught me how to build walls and call them independence.
You showed me beauty,
but you also taught me that here, love rarely stays—
because everyone is always looking for the next,
the better, the brighter thing.
I gave you my years, my energy, my heart.
And in return, you gave me a life I will never forget.
But I can't love you like this anymore.
I need softness. I need air. I need a love that stays.
Goodbye, New York.
You will always be the city that made me.
And the city I finally had to leave to save myself."

✦ ✦ ✦

"Every goodbye to a place is really a hello to yourself.
And sometimes the bravest thing you can do is walk
away from the city you thought was forever."

Chapter 42

Let the Garden Bloom

"There will come a day when the weight you've carried becomes the wings you fly with. Keep going. You're not behind. You're just becoming who you were always meant to be."

For far too long, I held everything inside. The pain. The heartbreak. The disappointments. The words I was too scared to speak. The emotions I was told were too much. The parts of me I thought no one could ever love.

I kept performing, pleasing, chasing love like it was something I had to earn. I lived a life built around expectations, not truth. A life that looked fine on the outside—but felt like suffocation on the inside.

I was surviving, not living. Existing, not breathing.

Until one day… I stopped. I let go. I surrendered.

I stopped begging for things not meant for me. I stopped carrying people who wouldn't carry me back. I stopped trying to control everything and finally allowed myself to feel everything.

And in that surrender, I found freedom.

I realized I don't have to prove my worth to be worthy. I don't have to chase love to deserve it. I don't have to shrink, hide, or silence my truth to be accepted. I just have to be me. Fully. Freely. Unapologetically.

We all have a choice. To stop living for approval. To stop betraying ourselves just to feel accepted. To stop watering gardens that were never meant to bloom.

Instead— Water your own. Tend to your heart like it matters. Because it does.

When you choose yourself, when you love yourself, when you commit to your own joy—everything changes. Your energy shifts. Your light grows stronger.

And suddenly, you start attracting what's meant for you— not through force, but through alignment. Because what is meant for you will never need to be chased. It will feel like home. It will come in peace. It will stay.

So let your garden bloom. Let it be wild. Let it be colorful. Let it be real. And watch the butterflies come.

Live boldly. Speak your truth. Laugh so hard you cry. Cry so hard you heal.

Say yes to things that set your soul on fire. Say no to anything that dims your light.

This life is yours. Not theirs. Yours.

So don't waste another moment trying to be anything but you. You are enough. You are worthy. You are already becoming everything you were always meant to be

I found my freedom the moment I stopped hiding my truth.

This story isn't perfect, but it's mine— and that is more than enough.

For far too long, I kept everything inside— every feeling, every wound, every unspoken word. I held on to people I should've released, to stories I should've let end, to pain that had long outlived its purpose.

But I didn't know how to let go. So I carried it all. I carried memories like weights. I carried silence like armor. And it was slowly destroying me.

I knew I couldn't heal if I kept pretending I was fine. I knew I couldn't move forward while chained to the past.

So I made a choice. To let it out. All of it.

And that's when this book was born.

The moment I wrote my first truth onto the page—something shifted. It wasn't dramatic. It wasn't sudden. But it was real.

It was like a crack of light in a tunnel I didn't even know I was buried in. Writing became my release. My freedom. The key that opened the prison I had built around myself— a prison made of fear, shame, silence, and self-protection.

But now… I'm no longer afraid. I'm no longer hiding.

This book is the door I walked through to come back to myself

In these pages, I told the truth—my truth. I wrote about heartbreak, betrayal, loneliness. But also about love, beauty, joy, and the moments that saved me.

I didn't write this to get revenge. Or to point fingers. I wrote this to be free. To finally let myself feel without apology. To honor the version of me that stayed quiet for far too long.

And no—I don't regret a single word. Because these are my feelings. This is my story. And I'm allowed to tell it.

I know the people I wrote about might remember things differently. They're allowed to. Their pain is real, too. Their perspective is theirs, just like mine is mine.

We are all living different truths, shaped by our own fears, wounds, and hopes. We are all just doing the best we can. And that—that should be enough.

I didn't write this book to be perfect. I wrote it to be honest. To say:

This is what it felt like to be me.

And maybe… If someone else out there is carrying the weight of unsaid feelings, If someone else is quietly breaking under the pressure of holding it all in, this book might help them find the courage to let it out, too.

Because our stories matter. Our voices matter. And we are not alone. Not anymore. Not ever again

So take this story and let it remind you— your truth is not too much. Your heart is not too broken. Your dreams are not too late. You are not too far gone.

You are right on time. You are allowed to bloom.

And if no one else has told you this yet— I'm proud of you.

Thank you for reading. Thank you for feeling. Thank you for walking this road with me.

Now go live. Fully. Wildly. Truthfully.

Let your own garden bloom and let this be your reminder: even after the longest winter, the flowers always return. ✣

✦　✦　✦

"Every ending is only a seed. Plant it. Water it. Trust it.
One day, it will grow into the life you've been waiting for."

Epilogue

The Garden After the Storm

There was a time I thought healing would mean forgetting. That I'd have to erase him, erase the pain, erase the versions of myself I no longer recognized. But healing didn't ask me to forget. It asked me to remember—and to let those memories change shape.

I no longer carry them as wounds. I carry them as roots. Proof that even when life breaks you, something new can grow in the cracks.

F is still part of my story. So are the heartbreaks, the silences, the nights I thought I wouldn't make it through. They are not my shame anymore. They are my soil. And from that soil, I've built something stronger: compassion, boundaries, love that begins with myself.

I don't know if we ever really stop grieving the people who marked us so deeply. Maybe the point isn't to stop grieving. Maybe the point is to learn how to live alongside it—how to build joy even with a scar, how to bloom even with the ache still humming quietly in the background.

If you've read this far, maybe you're carrying your own scars. Maybe you've been waiting for someone to tell you what I once needed to hear:

You are not broken beyond repair. You are not unworthy of love. And you are not alone.

There will be days when the silence feels heavy. When you wonder if hope is dangerous. When you're tempted to believe you'll never feel whole again. But trust this: the heart has a way of stitching itself back together, even when you're not watching.

One morning, you'll wake up and notice the light falls differently. That you breathe a little easier. That you laugh without thinking. That life doesn't feel like survival anymore—it feels like possibility.

And when that day comes, you'll know what I learned: Surrender is not defeat. It's the beginning.

So let the garden bloom. Because you survived the storm.

✦ ✦ ✦

"I didn't get the ending I hoped for, but I found something greater—myself. And maybe that's what surrender truly means: not giving up on love, but giving in to truth. To stand in the ruins of almost and still choose to bloom."

Acknowledgments

✦ ✦ ✦

This book would not exist without the people who stood with me when I couldn't stand on my own—when life felt too heavy, when silence pressed against my chest, and when I no longer trusted my own strength.

To my family and friends—thank you for holding space for me in ways both visible and invisible. For the patience that asked nothing of me when I had nothing to give, for the love that wrapped around me when I couldn't feel my own, and for the quiet encouragement that became the scaffolding I leaned on when my world was collapsing. You reminded me that even when everything else is uncertain, love can be steady.

Agnieszka and Daniel, you opened your door and your home to me when I had nowhere else to go. You stood by me and supported me when I needed it the most. You proved, in every action, that family is everything. I will never forget that.

Marie, you were the lighthouse when the storm felt endless. You showed me that true friendship is not measured by the years we've known someone, but by the courage to stand beside them when the ground is shaking. You reminded me that sometimes the most un-expected people become the greatest gifts, and that real friendship doesn't rescue you—it teaches you how to swim toward the shore when you think you're drowning.

To the friends who chose to stay—you taught me that "home" isn't always a place. It's the faces that keep showing up, again and again, even when it's messy, even when it's inconvenient, even when all you have to offer is your quiet presence. Thank you for choosing me, not just in the easy moments, but in the ones that scared me most.

Aric and Keith, you supported me all the way. You stood by me in the best and worst moments, you were my voice of reason when I couldn't hear my own, and you had the courage to tell me when I was wrong while still standing firmly by me when I was right. That balance, that honesty, and that loyalty are gifts I'll carry with me forever.

Ewelina, you are and will always be my dear friend, someone I love unconditionally. From the very beginning of our journey in New York, we connected in a way that words can never fully capture. You have stood by me through every season, supporting me without question, and reminding me what lifelong friendship truly means.

To the *Foreigner* family—especially the band and the management—thank you for welcoming me into your world with open arms, for your support, and for believing in me. For the laughs, the unforgettable memories, and for treating me like family when I needed it most. Stewart and Phil, thank you for seeing me, believing in me, and giving me a chance. Even after I left, your support never stopped. I carry deep gratitude for you, always.

To every soul who ever whispered "me too" after hearing my story—you are the reason I kept writing. You turned my loneliness into connection and gave meaning to my pain. Every time you shared your truth with me, it stitched another piece of hope into my own brokenness.

And to F.—thank you for the love that broke me open, for the silence that forced me to hear my own heart, and for the shadow and the light you left behind. Without you, this story would not have been born. This book carries both the ache of your absence and the beauty of what your presence once awakened in me. In some way, it will always carry you.

And finally, to future readers: wherever you are, holding this book—I hope it reminds you that even in the breaking, you are never truly alone.

Thank you, all of you, for teaching me that surrender is not about losing, but about finally learning how to be free.

This book is my surrender. My hope is that, in some small way, it helps you find yours.

About the Author

✦ ✦ ✦

Nobody is the pen name of **Mariusz Podkalicki**, a writer whose words were born in the quiet space between heartbreak and healing. For years, he carried silence—burying grief, love, and unanswered questions—until writing became the only way to survive them. On the page, he found not just expression, but transformation: a way to stitch himself back together, sentence by sentence.

Surrender is his debut memoir—an intimate and unflinching exploration of love, loss, and the long road back to self. It is a book about heartbreak, but also about the beauty that can emerge in its aftermath: resilience, clarity, and the quiet strength that comes from letting go. With raw honesty and lyrical reflection, Mariusz opens the door to moments most of us keep hidden, reminding readers that even in silence, none of us are ever truly alone.

Born in Poland and moving to the United States at nineteen with nothing but determination and a suitcase, Mariusz spent nearly two decades working as a personal and executive assistant to high-profile clients. Behind the glamour of that world, however, he faced his own battles—with identity, mental health, chronic illness, and the ache of loving too deeply. Those lived experiences shaped both the voice and the vulnerability found in his work.

Beyond writing, he draws inspiration from travel, music, and the small rituals of daily life—morning coffee, late-night journaling, walks through the city that raised and tested him. He is deeply passionate about mental health, self-acceptance, and using storytelling as a bridge between people: a way to remind us that even in our most private struggles, connection and healing are possible.

He publishes under his independent imprint, **The Nobody Collective**, dedicated to creating honest, heart-centered work that gives voice to the unspoken and light to the unseen.

Thank You

✦ ✦ ✦

To you— the one who made it all the way here. Thank you. Thank you for holding space for these pages, for walking through the heartbreak, the silence, the softness, and the scars with me. Whether you read this in one sitting or over many quiet nights, whether you cried, paused, or smiled somewhere in between—I'm grateful.

This book was never meant to be perfect. It was meant to be *honest*. And if something in it resonated with you—if you saw yourself between the lines or felt a flicker of recognition in the ache—then we've already shared something deeply human. And that means everything to me.

I didn't write this book as a lesson. I wrote it as a mirror. A place to put what was too heavy to carry alone. A place to remember that even when things fall apart, we don't have to.

If you're still healing—take your time. If you're still searching—keep going. If you're still holding on—know that it's okay to let go. And if you're rebuilding—brick by tender brick—I hope this reminded you that you're not alone.

Thank you for being here. For seeing me. For letting me be part of your story, even for a little while.

With love and deepest gratitude,

Nobody-Mariusz Podkalicki

Resources

✦ ✦ ✦

If you are struggling, please know you are not alone. Healing is not a straight path, and reaching out for support is an act of strength—not weakness.

Mental Health & Crisis Support

United States
- 988 Suicide & Crisis Lifeline – Dial 988 anytime for free, confidential support.
- Crisis Text Line – Text HELLO to 741741 to connect with a trained counselor.
- The Trevor Project (LGBTQ+ support) – Call 1-866-488-7386 or text START to 678678.

United Kingdom
- Samaritans – Call 116 123 or visit samaritans.org.

Canada
- 988 Suicide Crisis Helpline – Dial 988.

International
- Visit findahelpline.com to find crisis hotlines and mental health resources available in your country.

Chronic Illness & Support Communities

- National Alliance on Mental Illness (NAMI) – nami.org | Education, resources, and support groups.

- Mental Health America (MHA) – mhanational.org | Screenings and peer support.
- Reddit & Peer Forums – Online spaces where people share lived experiences of heartbreak, depression, and chronic illness.

A Gentle Reminder

Reaching out does not make you weak. It makes you human. If this book has resonated with you, and if you ever find yourself on the edge of silence, I hope you remember there are voices waiting to listen, and hands ready to hold you through it.